healthy lunchboxes
for kids

Amanda Grant

photography by Tara Fisher

RYLAND
PETERS
& SMALL

Designer Iona Hoyle
Senior Editor Catherine Osborne
Production Manager Patricia Harrington
Art Director Leslie Harrington
Publishing Director Alison Starling
Food Stylists Amanda Grant and Jacque Malouf
Prop Stylist Liz Belton
Indexer Ann Barrett

First published in Great Britain in 2008

This paperback edition published in 2010
by Ryland Peters & Small
20–21 Jockey's Fields
London WC1R 4BW
www.rylandpeters.com

10 9 8 7 6 5 4 3 2 1

Text © Amanda Grant 2008, 2010
Design and photographs
© Ryland Peters & Small 2008, 2010

A CIP record of this book is available from the
British Library.

ISBN: 978 1 84975 048 6

Printed in China

Notes

- All spoon measurements are level unless otherwise specified.
- Ovens should be preheated to the specified temperatures. All ovens work slightly differently. We recommend using an oven thermometer and suggest you consult the maker's handbook for any special instructions, particularly if you are cooking in a fan-assisted oven, as you will need to adjust temperatures according to manufacturer's instructions.
- All eggs are medium, unless otherwise specified. Recipes containing raw or partially cooked egg, or raw fish or shellfish, should not be served to the very young, very old, anyone with a compromised immune system or pregnant women.

Neither the author nor the publisher can be held responsible for any claim arising out of the information in this book. Always consult your health visitor or doctor if you have any concerns about your child's health or nutrition.

contents

introduction

the perfect lunchbox

What foods should you pack into your child's lunchbox? If you're a busy parent, it can be challenging to come up with options that are nutritious, practical and affordable, and, most importantly, that children enjoy eating.

Some 5 million children's lunchboxes are prepared in British homes every weekday, and a Food Standards Agency survey revealed that 3 out of 4 of these were likely to contain foods that were too high in saturated fat, salt or sugar. The same survey indicated that almost half of these lunches failed to include any fruit. Most, however, did include crisps, chocolate, biscuits, sugary drinks and other heavily processed snacks.

A diet that is high in fat, salt and refined carbohydrates not only lays the foundations for heart disease and high blood pressure later in life, but can also contribute to reduced mental alertness, tiredness and lack of concentration in school.

Despite what many manufacturers promote, highly processed foods that are packaged in brightly coloured plastic are not what we should be giving our children. The food is often poor quality, and you are mostly paying for the elaborate packaging and advertising.

Instead, you can save money and give children a better start in life by providing them with good nutritious food. With some forethought and a little time, you can make a healthy lunchbox of fresh and unprocessed food – the sort of food that our parents grew up eating before manufacturers tapped into the children's snack-food market. Next time you have a

Sunday roast, for example, save some cold meat to put in lunchbox sandwiches on the following Monday.

Try to think of providing packed lunches as the perfect opportunity for setting some basic principles about eating good food, rather than seeing it as a chore. Lunch should provide children with approximately one third of their daily energy needs as well as one third of their required protein, carbohydrate, vitamin, mineral and fibre intake. Refer to page 14 for an example of the perfect healthy lunchbox, and use this as your guide to preparing achievable lunches each day. If you can feed your children a healthy diet 80 per cent of the time, then you are doing pretty well.

the perfect lunchbox

A perfect lunchbox should contain (see page 14 for further information):

- 1 serving of a protein-rich food
- 1 serving of carbohydrate or starchy food
- 1 serving of a calcium-rich food
- 1 serving of fruit
- 1 serving of vegetables
- 1 drink

'fast'-food basics

Before you start reading about how to make a healthy lunchbox, don't forget that children need a nutritious breakfast before they go to school. This meal needs to provide them with enough energy to get them through the morning. High-sugar breakfasts, like cereals coated in sugar, are best avoided because they will only provide short-lived energy. Instead, start the day with porridge made with low-fat milk, muesli with semi-skimmed milk or wholegrain toast with some scrambled egg, or peanut butter.

Continue on the right path by packing some healthy mid-morning snacks in your child's lunchbox that provide slow-release energy, like fresh fruit or vegetables, cereal bars or rice cakes with dip (see pages 92–93). To help keep your child's mood and behaviour on an even keel, and to help him/her concentrate in class during the afternoon, make sure you provide a nutritionally balanced lunchbox.

The 'Balance of Good Health' guidelines developed by the Food Standards Agency can help in making healthy food choices.

protein foods

Foods in this group include meat, chicken, fish, eggs, beans, lentils and nuts. These are high protein foods and are vital for our child's growth and brain development. A popular myth is that the more protein you give children, the quicker they will grow and develop, but this isn't the case. Protein is made up of building blocks called amino acids, of which there are 22. Most of these can be made in our body from proteins except for an essential 8 (or 9 in children) that must come from our food.

Protein is either animal-based or vegetable-based. Animal proteins, such as chicken, fish, meat and eggs, contain all the essential amino acids. Plant proteins are referred to as incomplete proteins because they don't contain all of these amino acids. If you wish to feed your child a vegetarian diet, you will need to make sure that it is a combination of grains, nuts, seeds, pulses and beans to give a complete balance of these essential amino acids. Protein-rich foods are also good sources of some B vitamins, iron and zinc.

protein requirement

Every packed lunch should contain 1 serving of food from the meat, fish and alternatives group. As a rule, children need 2 servings of these foods each day. Children who are vegetarian generally need 3 servings.

For children aged 5–8 years, a serving is:
- 1 slice lean cooked meat
- 2 thin slices cooked poultry
- ½ fillet fish
- 1 egg
- 2 tablespoons lentils or beans

For children aged 9–11 years, a serving is:
- 2 slices lean meat
- 2 slices poultry
- 1 fillet fish
- 1–2 eggs
- 3 tablespoons lentils or beans

***Note:** For fish and egg recipes see pages 32, 35, 40, 43, 80–82.

carbohydrate foods

These provide a steady stream of energy and help keep sugar levels balanced. They are typically found in unrefined and wholegrain foods, which are richer in nutrients and fibre than their refined equivalents. Good slow-release carbohydrates include oats, wholewheat breads and baked products, brown rice, wholewheat pasta and potatoes with skins.

<hr>

carbohydrate requirement

Every packed lunch should contain 1 or more servings of foods from the bread, potatoes and other cereals group (depending on how much is provided in other meals). As a rule, children need 4–6 servings a day.

For children aged 5–8 years, a serving may be:

- 1 small slice bread
- ½ small roll
- 1 medium potato
- 3 tablespoons pasta or rice
- 3 tablespoons breakfast cereal

For children aged 9–11 years, a serving may be:

- 1 slice bread
- 1 roll
- 1 medium potato
- 4 tablespoons pasta or rice
- 4 tablespoons breakfast cereal

* **Note:** For potato, pasta and cereal recipes see pages 42–45 and 120.

<hr>

Fast-releasing carbohydrates, on the other hand, include high-sugar foods made with lots of unrefined sugar, like biscuits and cakes, and baked goods that contain high fat and white flour, like croissants.

It is fine to include some fast-releasing carbohydrates in your child's diet, but to help slow down the rate at which they rush through the bloodstream it is a good idea to combine them with protein-rich food. For example, white rice is best served with chicken or fish. This is simply because proteins take a longer time to digest and hence slow down the absorption of the fast-releasing sugars.

As a general guide, children over the age of 5 years should be eating two thirds wholegrain foods, like wholewheat pasta and wholewheat bread, and one third white flour, pasta, rice, etc. Make sure you include slow-release carbohydrates in your child's diet.

fibre

If you increase the number of slow-release carbohydrates in your child's diet, you will also increase their fibre intake. Fibre is important for a number of reasons – it maintains the health of the digestive tract, slows down the release of sugars into the bloodstream, helps the body eliminate toxins and feeds beneficial bacteria that are found in the gut.

If children are fed a processed diet that is high in refined foods, and hence less fibre, they are more likely to suffer from constipation. Sadly, this is a side effect of the modern diet that is becoming more prevalent, so much so that constipation clinics for children have been set up.

fruit and vegetables

Everyone knows about the recommended 5 a day, but perhaps not everyone realizes that this includes frozen, dried and tinned fruit. The average fruit and vegetable consumption among British children is 2 servings a day – a long way from the recommended 5.

Fruit and vegetables are a great source of vitamins, minerals and fibre. Children need them in their diet to help boost their immune system. Fruits that are especially rich in immune-boosting vitamin C include oranges, kiwi fruit, strawberries and raspberries. It is also believed that eating fresh fruits and vegetables during childhood can help reduce the risk of cancer, heart disease and stroke later in life.

Every packed lunch should ideally have 1 piece of fruit and a serving of vegetables. To help your child reach the 5-a-day target, make sure that at each meal and snack (which makes a total of 5) he/she is eating 1 serving of fruit or vegetables. To make it more interesting, serve different colours each time and let your child be involved in the preparation as much as possible.

fruit & vegetable requirement

Children need 3 servings of vegetables a day. A rough guide to 1 serving of vegetables is approximately the amount a child can hold in his/her hand:

Vegetables
For children aged 5–8 years, a serving is:
- 1 small carrot
- 2 tablespoons small vegetables (such as sweetcorn)
- 3 or 4 cherry tomatoes

For children aged 9–11 years, a serving is:
- 1 carrot
- 3 tablespoons small vegetables (such as sweetcorn)
- 5 cherry tomatoes

Children need 2–3 servings of fruit a day. A rough guide to 1 serving of fruit is approximately the amount a child can hold in his/her hand:

Fruit
For children aged 5–8 years, a serving is:
- 1 small fruit, such as a plum
- 1 kiwi fruit
- 1 satsuma
- 6 strawberries
- a big handful of tinned or dried fruit
- 1 small glass fruit juice

For children aged 9–11 years, a serving is:
- 1–2 small fruits like a plum, kiwi fruit, or satsuma
- 10 strawberries
- a big handful of tinned or dried fruit
- 1 glass fruit juice

*__Note:__ Raw fruit and vegetables have the most nutrients, so include some in your child's lunchbox. Avoid giving too much juice as it is high in sugar (see page 12).

calcium

Calcium is vital for healthy bones and teeth and is also involved in maintaining normal nerve and muscle function. Good calcium-rich foods include cheese, milk, yoghurt, soya milk (if fortified with calcium), soya yoghurt, sardines (with bones mashed in) and nuts (especially almonds). These foods are also high in protein.

Try as much as possible to avoid buying yoghurts or fromage frais that are high in sugar, and avoid any with artificial sweeteners, colours and flavours. Try adding fresh fruit purées to give flavour. Home-made milkshakes or smoothies can also be a great way of adding calcium to your child's diet, especially if he/she is not keen on drinking milk or eating yoghurt. Avoid any cheese brands that are marketed at children. Although they contain the same amount of calcium as real cheese, they are also often laden with additives and salt.

calcium requirement

Children need 3 servings of food from the milk, cheese and yoghurt group or other high calcium foods a day. See below for guides:

For children aged 5–8 years, a serving is:
- 1 small cup of milk
- 1 pot of yoghurt
- a handful of cheese
- 1–2 tinned sardines (with bones mashed)

For children aged 9–11 years, a serving is:
- 1 medium cup of milk
- 1 pot of yoghurt
- a handful of cheese
- 2 tinned sardines (with bones mashed)

salt

Children are vulnerable to the side effects of too much salt in their diet, and should limit their intake. In addition to adding salt at the table with a salt shaker, the obvious foods that have high salt levels include crisps and salted nuts. Salt is also found in foods where you might not expect it, such as cereal bars, baked goods, tinned foods (tuna in brine, soup, baked beans), processed meats (salami, bacon), and sauces (soy sauce, tomato ketchup). Make sure you check the labels on these foods (see below), especially as some can exceed your child's daily salt intake. Even better, make your own home-made foods, such as soup and beans, and don't add salt.

salt intake

Aim to keep salt intake below the following:
for children aged 4–6 years: 3 g per day
for children aged 7–10 years: 5 g per day
for children aged 11–14 years: 6 g per day

*Note: Sadly, the reality is that many children in the UK are actually eating more like 10–12 g per day.

The Food Standards Agency recommends that you look at the labels on food and use the following amounts as a guide to help you decide whether it contains too much salt or not:

- In 100 g of food:
  more than 1.25 g is high
  less than 0.25 g is low

- Sodium: 1 g of sodium is equivalent to 2.5 g of salt:
  more than 0.5 g is high
  less than 0.1 g is low

sugar

Like salt, too much refined sugar can be bad for children. Refined sugar provides very little nutrition, except calories. Unrefined sugar (natural brown sugar) does provide a few nutrients, but should still be kept to a sensible limit. A much healthier option is food that naturally contains sugar, like fresh fruit, which also contains fibre and vitamins to promote health.

There are lots of obvious foods that contain sugar, but there are also many foods that contain hidden sugars. You will probably be surprised to learn that many yoghurts (especially brands marketed at children), cereals and baked beans contain quite a lot of sugar.

It is believed that too much sugar in your child's diet can cause swings in blood sugar levels, which can lead to poor concentration, bad behaviour and low energy levels, although this is still being researched. It is also a major contributor to tooth decay and obesity. The World Health Organization recommends that adults and children should get no more than 10 per cent of their calories from sugar.

Keep your child's sugar intake to a minimum by giving him/her lots of fresh fruit and vegetables. You can also make cakes and biscuits at home, so you know how much sugar has gone into the food. Many recipes can easily have the amount of sugar reduced. If you want to give your child a piece of cake or a cereal bar that contains sugar, it is best to give this as part of a meal. This is because during a meal the amount of saliva in the mouth increases, therefore making it easier to wash the food, and sugar, away from the teeth.

Children don't need to have a sweet treat in their packed lunch every day – vary it with natural yoghurt mixed with muesli, puréed fruit or a handful of dried fruits. Even though dried fruits contain high amounts of natural sugar, they are slow-releasing especially when combined with a slow-release carbohydrate (see page 121 for Apricot Slices as an example).

Try not to add sugar to food unless absolutely necessary. Even fruits that may taste slightly sour to you can taste sweet to children, especially if they are not used to eating lots of sweet foods. Limit processed foods that may contain lots of unnecessary sugar and keep to low-sugar snacks, like rice cakes, oat cakes, fruit, vegetables and popcorn.

sugar intake

Aim to keep sugar intake below the following:
for children aged 4–6 years: 40 g (2½ tablespoons) per day

for children aged 7–10 years: 46 g (3 tablespoons) per day

for children aged 11–14 years: 50 g (3½ tablespoons) per day

The Food Standards Agency recommends that:
- In 100 g of food:
  more than 10 g is high
  less than 2 g is low

*Note: Check food labels for the following – sucrose, glucose, dextrose, fruit syrup (fructose) and glucose, which are all forms of sugar.

fats

Children need some fat for optimum health. It is particularly important that a child's diet includes 'good' fats, but limits the 'bad' fats.

The best fats are monounsaturated and polyunsaturated fats. Monounsaturated fats are found in olive oil, almonds, almond oil, peanuts, hazelnuts, avocados and olives. These are believed to help keep cholesterol levels low and reduce the risk of heart disease and cancer in later life. Many of these foods are also good sources of vitamin E, an important antioxidant.

Polyunsaturated fats include omega-3 and omega-6 essential fatty acids. Omega-3 fatty acids provide the essential fatty acid alpha linolenic acid and are found in walnuts, walnut oil, flax (or linseed), and oily fish (mackerel, herring, sardines, salmon, fresh tuna and trout). These fats are very important for brain development, and some studies have suggested that poor concentration in schoolchildren may be linked to low intakes of these omega-3 fatty acids in their diet. Omega-6 fatty acids are most common in nuts, seeds and their oils (e.g. sunflower oil, sesame oil) and contain the essential fatty acid linoleic acid. They are also important in many aspects of growth and brain development. Omega-6 fats should be balanced with omega-3 fats and not taken excessively.

Minimize saturated fats in your child's diet and try to avoid trans fats. Saturated fats are found naturally in animal product, such as meat and butter, whereas trans fats are formed when healthy unsaturated oils are changed during hydrogenation, a process that is used to harden liquid vegetable oils into solids. These fats are often found in margarines and processed foods, such as cakes, biscuits and crisps. A small amount of saturated fat in the diet is reasonable.

High intakes of these fats (saturated and trans) are associated with the development of atherosclerosis (fatty deposits in the arteries), which can lead to heart disease and stroke. They may also be a risk factor in the development of other diseases, such as cancer and, when combined with a high calorie diet, obesity.

To help increase the good fats in your child's diet, try to cook with olive or canola oil, and use other nut and seed oils, such as walnut or flaxseed oil to make salad dressings. Flaxseed oil is available in some supermarkets and healthfood stores. Try adding it to smoothies or yoghurts. Sneak seeds into your child's diet by including them as snack items in his/her lunchbox or by adding them to baked goods. Also, including oily fish in your child's diet each week provides a good source of protein as well as a healthy boost of omega-3 fats.

fat intake

Try to avoid adding excess fat to your child's diet, aim to use small amounts of healthy fats for cooking and spreads and include at least 1 serving a week (60–80 g) of oily fish and some of the foods listed below.

For children aged 5–8 years try to include the following each day:
- 1 tablespoon nuts and seeds
- 2 teaspoons nut or seed oils

For children aged 9–11 years try to include the following each day:
- 1 heaped tablespoon nuts and seeds
- 1 tablespoon nut or seed oils

what to drink

When it comes to drinks, water is best. Children should take a bottle of water to school with them every day. Most children do not drink enough water and a high percentage of schoolchildren are dehydrated. When your child becomes dehydrated, it has a negative impact on his/her ability to concentrate in class. Some schools have even started to have water dispensers installed to encourage children to drink more. Similarly, some teachers are recognizing that it is a good idea to allow children to keep bottles of water in their classroom.

If children are reluctant to drink plain water, which is often the case, or if they have become used to drinking juices or squash, you will need to work hard at encouraging them to drink it. Only give them water to take to school, with the occasional fruit smoothie or juice in their lunchbox. Pack fun-coloured straws and, if that doesn't work, fill up bottles with water and then ask your child to decorate them with his/her favourite stickers.

If you want to give your child fresh fruit juice, pack a small bottle with his/her lunch, but explain that he/she will still need to drink water during the rest of the day. Water should be the drink children automatically ask for when they are thirsty. You should only give them fruit juice occasionally. Children can easily consume large amounts of juice, which will reduce their appetite for other foods and provide excess calories. A good guide is to limit to one drink of juice a day.

why water?

Children need water to:
- help keep them hydrated
- help with concentration and memory
- help aid digestion and absorption
- help prevent constipation
- eliminate toxins from the body
- maintain body temperature (for example, if children have been playing sport on a hot day, they need water to help their bodies cool down).

how to involve your children

There is no doubt in my mind that children who help with choosing food and preparing it are more likely to enjoy eating it. Believe it or not, involving them can actually help you too, and doesn't always involve a lot of mess.

Children can help with simple tasks that will save you time and make them feel involved, such as peeling and washing carrots, counting out fruit and putting it into pots, and choosing dried fruits and mixing them together.

At weekends, when you have more time to spend in the kitchen, ask them to help make food that can go in the freezer. Tarts, muffins, flapjacks, cakes and cookies can all be made and frozen, allowing you to take one out at a time to put in your child's packed lunch. You can even put frozen food into your child's packed lunch – it should have thawed by lunchtime, and it will help to keep other foods in the lunchbox fresh.

If your child is particularly fussy about food, come to an arrangement where there may be something in the lunchbox that he/she chooses and something that you choose. Write the occasional note and put it inside your child's lunchbox so he/she knows you are thinking of them. Write something funny that will make your child relax and perhaps encourage him/her to eat his/her lunch. Help your child enjoy lunchtime, so that it's something to look forward to rather than a chore. It may take a bit of effort on your part, but the end result is very satisfying for both parent and child.

growing curly cress

Growing your own cress is just one inventive way to get your children involved with making their own packed lunches (see opposite).

how to grow cress

1 Purchase a packet of seeds from your local garden centre or supermarket.

2 Find a suitable container and line it with kitchen roll, cotton wool or a thick layer of seed compost.

3 Moisten the kitchen roll with water and sprinkle the seeds over the top.

4 Cover with kitchen roll until the seeds start to germinate, then remove.

5 It's important to keep the cress moist, so sprinkle with water when needed.

6 Cut the cress with scissors when it's about 5 cm high. The cress should take up to 14 days to reach this height.

7 Put the cress in a sandwich of your choice (see egg and cress sandwich idea on page 32).

the perfect lunchbox

You are certainly not alone if you struggle to think of things to put into your child's lunchbox. Once you have managed to gather together some bits and pieces, you may still be left wondering whether the lunch will provide your child with enough of the right nutrients. You may also be unsure as to whether he/she will actually eat the food that you have given him/her.

Sadly, studies have shown that many lunchboxes contain double the recommended daily amount of sugar and nearly half the safe daily intake for salt and saturated fats. Popular items found in children's lunchboxes include chocolate bars and packets of crisps, and very few contain fresh fruit.

A good lunchbox should provide your child with enough energy to sustain him/her all afternoon. It should provide approximately one third of the recommended daily energy needs, as well as approximately one third of the daily protein, carbohydrate, fibre, vitamin and mineral requirements. Making a balanced lunchbox is surprisingly easy to achieve. Opposite is a simple checklist to get you started.

- **fruit**
1 serving of fresh or dried fruit

- **vegetables**
1 serving of vegetables or salad (e.g. carrots, celery, peppers, cucumber)

- **dairy**
1 item from this group, such as cheese, yoghurt, milk OR alternatively another calcium-rich food, such as calcium-fortified soya, tofu, tinned fish, like pilchards and sardines (the edible bones are a good source of calcium) and nuts.

- **protein**
1 serving of food from the meat, fish or alternative group of protein-rich foods.

- **carbohydrate**
1 or more servings of foods from the bread, potato and other cereals group.

- **drink**
A drink – approximately 200-300 ml. This should preferably be water.

sandwiches

breads

There are hundreds of different types of bread available in supermarkets today. It is no longer just a case of choosing between a white, wholemeal or brown loaf. There are breads made from mixed grains, those that have been bran-enriched or fortified with vitamins and minerals, as well as fruit breads, seed breads and nut breads. Bread also comes sliced, unsliced, wrapped, unwrapped, part-baked and frozen.

There are different shaped breads, including the cob, cottage, barrel, bloomer, batch, sandwich and farmhouse. There are also baguettes and croissants, pita bread, ciabatta, bagels and naan. The choice is enormous, and they are all good for children.

If your child demands white bread sandwiches, my advice is to persevere and slowly introduce your child to different breads. It is our job, as parents, to encourage our children to try different food.

White bread is made with white flour, which has had most of its fibre and some of its minerals and vitamins removed, and has sometimes been bleached or refined. It is fine to include some white bread in your child's diet, especially as it's often been fortified with calcium and niacin (a vitamin that aids the removal of toxic chemicals from the body), but make sure you also introduce other breads to your child's lunchbox. As a general guide, children over the age of 5 can have two-thirds wholemeal or brown bread and one third white bread in their diet.

The sandwich recipes in the following chapter do not list the type of bread that should be used – on the whole, it is up to you to choose. Occasionally, suggestions have been made where a particular bread may work best.

▪ loaves – wholemeal, granary, seed, herb & tomato bread
Experiment with different types of bread each week; your child will enjoy his/her sandwiches more as a result. You may discover that your child will eat items in bread, such as tomatoes, that he/she wouldn't usually eat raw.

▪ pita bread
This is a flat bread traditionally from Greece and the Middle East. Children love pita breads for their pocket-like effect, and they often come in small sizes as well as large. Children particularly like them lightly toasted before they are filled.

▪ tortilla wraps
Made from wheat flour, these are ideal for wrapping soft ingredients, like cream cheese and peanut butter, and are easy for children to eat.

▪ rolls
Available in many varieties (white, brown, granary, topped with seeds) and different shapes and sizes, you will often find that children are happier with small soft rolls because they are easier for them to eat.

▪ French bread
Some children find French bread takes too long to eat because of its hard outer crust, and don't finish it. French bread requires quite a lot of chewing, so children often get bored and play with their friends instead. It would be great if schools encouraged children to stay sitting until everyone had finished eating, but because this isn't often the case it's best to give younger children soft rolls, which are more manageable.

▪ bagels
There are a variety of different bagel flavours available, and they are popular with children because of their slightly soft texture.

▪ ciabatta
A crusty white bread often identified by its shape, which resembles a flattened slipper, and thus the meaning of the word 'ciabatta' in Italian. The great thing about ciabatta is that you can often buy it part-baked, which is ideal for keeping in the freezer until you need it.

▪ focaccia
A soft white Italian bread made with white flour and olive oil, often topped with onions, herbs or other foodstuffs. It looks a bit like a thick pizza base.

▪ fruit bread
These are quite popular among young children because they have a hint of sweetness. Try spreading these breads with cream cheese.

cheese sandwiches

cheddar with spring onion & tomato

Grate a chunk of Cheddar into a bowl, add ¼ spring onion (finely chopped) and 1 ripe tomato (finely chopped). Mix the ingredients together and put into 2 rolls or pitas of your choice.

ploughman's

Most children love this popular combination, and it's healthy for them. Put a big handful of grated Cheddar into a roll or your chosen bread, add 1 teaspoon chutney, 1 chopped tomato and top with a handful of finely chopped lettuce.

cheese & beetroot

Thinly slice a small piece of Cheddar and place onto your chosen bread. Top with an equal amount of thinly sliced raw beetroot. You can also grate both of these if you think your child would prefer it.

cheese & apple

Grate a chunk of your child's favourite hard cheese and mix it with grated apple, 1 chopped spring onion, a squeeze of lemon and a little mayonnaise. This combination is particularly good in wholemeal bread or rolls. If you want to add a bit more protein, you could also add a few chopped nuts.

Greek sandwiches

Mix together some crumbled feta cheese with 3–4 black olives (stones removed) and a chopped ripe tomato. Spread onto your chosen bread.

cream cheese & spinach

Spread some cream cheese onto a flour tortilla, top with 1 handful of washed baby spinach leaves (pick off any tough stalks), and then carefully roll the tortilla. Cut into 3 pieces, so that you have 3 easy-to-hold sandwiches.

note: all sandwiches make 1 unless otherwise stated.

cream cheese & sun-dried tomatoes

Spread some cream cheese onto your chosen bread, and top with a 1–2 finely chopped sun-dried tomatoes.

cream cheese & red pepper

Spread some cream cheese onto your chosen bread and then scatter over ¼ red pepper (finely chopped). Alternatively, use a roasted red pepper from a jar, slice and scatter over the cheese.

cream cheese & pesto

Spread some cream cheese onto your chosen bread and then spread a small amount of red or green pesto on top.

cream cheese & pear

Spread some cream cheese onto your chosen bread and then thinly slice ½ pear and cover with a little lemon juice. Put the pear on top of the cheese.

cream cheese & cucumber

Spread some cream cheese onto your chosen bread and top with thinly sliced cucumber.

cream cheese & avocado

Spread some cream cheese onto your chosen bread, top with ½ avocado (sliced or roughly mashed with a few drops of lemon juice to prevent it from turning brown), and sprinkle with a few poppy seeds, if liked. Grated carrot and cream cheese also make a good combination.

cottage cheese & pineapple

Mix together 2 tablespoons cottage cheese with a few pieces of chopped tinned pineapple. Spoon onto your chosen bread.

cottage cheese & fruit

Mix together 2 tablespoons cottage cheese with a few raisins and finely chopped dried apricots – or any other dried fruits. Spoon into a roll.

houmous sandwiches

You can either make your own houmous or buy it. Avoid buying low-fat houmous because it often contains hydrogenated fats, which can raise cholesterol levels in the blood and are best avoided. You can combine houmous with all kinds of ingredients to add flavour and texture and then spread onto sandwiches, or serve as a dip with vegetable sticks.

houmous & grated carrot

Spread some houmous onto your chosen bread, and top with a peeled and grated carrot.

houmous & grated Cheddar

Spread some houmous onto your chosen bread, and add a handful of grated Cheddar cheese.

houmous & avocado

Spread some houmous onto your chosen bread. Mash ½ ripe avocado with a few drops of lemon juice to prevent discolouration. Spread the avocado on top of the houmous.

houmous & beetroot

Spread some houmous onto your chosen bread, and grate a little raw beetroot over the top.

houmous, tomatoes & lettuce

Spread some houmous onto your chosen bread, and top with slices of tomato and lettuce leaves.

If you want to make your own home-made houmous, see page 92.

nutrition tip Even if your child is not vegetarian, try to include some vegetable protein foods in his/her diet, like chickpeas, as they provide a great type of fibre that is beneficial to the digestive system.

vegetarian sandwiches

If you are feeding your child a vegetarian diet, you need to make sure he/she gets all the essential nutrients usually provided in meat.

avocado & red pepper

Mash ½ ripe avocado with a little lemon juice, and spread onto your chosen bread. Finely chop ¼ pepper (orange, yellow and red are sweeter than green) and sprinkle over the top of the avocado. Alternatively, use a chopped roasted red pepper from a jar, sliced.

falafel in pita

Falafel is best served in pita, and is easy to eat and tastes great. This is a very quick and simple version of falafel, and is a good way to encourage your children to eat chickpeas.

makes 12

2 tablespoons olive oil

1 small onion, chopped

1 garlic clove, peeled and crushed

2 x 400-g tins chickpeas, washed and drained

1 teaspoon ground cumin

1 teaspoon ground coriander

a handful of freshly chopped coriander or mint

2 tablespoons mango chutney

freshly ground black pepper

plain flour, lightly seasoned

lettuce, shredded (optional)

1 tomato, sliced (optional)

Heat 1 tablespoon of the olive oil in a frying pan, add the onion and garlic and fry very gently until soft for approximately 5 minutes. Tip the onion and garlic into a bowl, add the chickpeas, cumin and ground coriander, then roughly whiz together with a hand-held blender.

Add the fresh coriander and mango chutney and season with freshly ground black pepper.

Mould the mixture into 12 balls and flatten into patty shapes. Dip them in the seasoned plain flour so they are lightly coated. Heat the remaining olive oil in the frying pan and fry the falafels on medium heat for 3 minutes on each side until golden brown. Leave to cool, then put into pita breads with the lettuce, tomato and extra mango chutney, if liked.

roast meats & bacon

One great thing about having a roast at the weekend is that you should have some leftover cold meat, ideal for packed lunches at the beginning of the week. A slice of meat counts as 1 portion of your child's daily protein requirement (see page 7).

roast beef with horseradish & cucumber

Some children love the taste of horseradish, others hate it and find it too hot. Spread a tiny amount of horseradish over your chosen bread, top with 2 pieces of roast beef and a few thin slices of cucumber.

roast pork with apple sauce

Most children love this combination. Finely chop 2 slices of cooked pork and mix with 2 tablespoons apple sauce. Spoon the mixture into a roll. Alternatively, split the roll, spread with apple sauce and fill with the pork. The apple sauce adds a wonderful sweetness and helps to bind the pork together.

roast pork with chutney

If your child likes chutney, mixing it with a cold meat is an easy Monday-morning sandwich filler. Spread some chutney onto your chosen bread and top with 2 slices of pork.

lamb with mint jelly & baby spinach

This may not sound like one of your typical sandwich fillings, but it just makes sense to use up leftover meats and mix them with their natural accompaniments. Spread some mint jelly onto your chosen bread. Top with 2 slices of leftover lamb and some baby spinach leaves, which are a great source of iron.

bacon with watercress & grated carrot

Finely chop 2 grilled unsmoked bacon rashers and put onto your chosen bread. Top with a handful of watercress and grated carrot.

grilled bacon with lettuce & tomato

With this combination, it works best if all the ingredients are finely chopped and mixed together, especially for younger children. Older children can manage eating bigger pieces of bacon with sliced tomatoes and shredded lettuce. Put 2 grilled unsmoked bacon rashers onto your chosen bread and top with slices of tomato and a little shredded lettuce.

bacon with egg & tomato

Mash 1 hard-boiled egg (see page 32), spread onto 2 slices of bread, sprinkle over 2 finely chopped grilled unsmoked bacon rashers and top with 1 ripe sliced tomato. This makes 2 sandwiches.

nutrition tip Always choose good-quality sausages; cheap sausages are packed with cheap fillers. For some extra-special sausages, try the sesame seed sausages on page 73. These are popular with adults, as well as children, and are perfect for birthday parties.

ham & sausages

ham with grated cheese

This is my middle daughter's all-round favourite sandwich, and she says it works best in a soft roll. Put 2 slices of ham into a roll and top with a handful of grated Cheddar.

ham with beetroot pickle

Spread a little beetroot (or other) pickle onto your chosen bread. Top with 2 slices of ham.

ham with tomato & shredded lettuce

Put 2 slices of ham into a roll and add 1 thinly sliced tomato and a little shredded lettuce. This is easier for a child to eat in a roll, because the filling is less likely to fall out.

cooked sausage & tomato

Thinly slice a cooked cold sausage. Spread some tomato ketchup onto your chosen bread and top with the sausage and 1 sliced tomato.

sausage & chutney

Thinly slice a cooked cold sausage. Spread some chutney onto your chosen bread and top with the sausage. Try the sesame seed sausages opposite if your child fancies something a little more exciting than plain sausages (see page 73).

chicken & turkey

chicken with mayonnaise, yoghurt, raisins & nuts

Finely dice 2 slices of cooked chicken breast and put into a bowl. Add a little mayonnaise, yoghurt, a handful of raisins (or cranberries) and a handful of chopped nuts. Mix together and spoon into a pita bread.

chicken with mango chutney & cucumber

Shred a little cooked chicken and put into a pita or roll, top with a dollop of mango chutney and some thinly sliced cucumber.

turkey with spring onions & apple sauce

Shred some cooked turkey meat. Spread a little apple sauce onto your chosen bread and scatter over the turkey. Top with ¼ chopped spring onion and cut into 2 sandwiches.

turkey with cranberry sauce & lettuce

Shred some cooked turkey meat. Spread some cranberry sauce onto a wrap and top with the turkey and shredded lettuce. If you make these wraps the night before, place a cocktail stick through them to hold them together. Remove the cocktail sticks before packing your child's lunch, and roll the wraps up in greaseproof paper.

nutrition tip Turkey is a good source of zinc – a mineral that helps aid digestion and maintain a healthy immune system. It is also important for healthy skin.

egg sandwiches

egg mayonnaise with watercress or lettuce

Hard boil an egg and lightly mash it in a bowl. Add 2 teaspoons mayonnaise or salad cream, and season with freshly ground black pepper. Mix together the ingredients, spoon into your chosen bread and add a handful of fresh watercress.

egg & cress

Has your child ever grown cress? It's fun and a great way to illustrate where food comes from. You will also find that your child is more willing to eat things that he/she has helped to grow (see page 13 for instructions).

Hard boil an egg and lightly mash it in a bowl. Add 2 teaspoons mayonnaise or salad cream. Spoon the mixture onto your chosen bread. Add a handful of your home-grown fresh cress, cutting from the bottom.

egg, bacon & tomato

If you don't already have some cooked bacon to hand, you will need to turn on the grill to make this sandwich, so you may as well grill at least enough bacon for 2 sandwiches to make it worthwhile. You do not need to add any mayonnaise or salad cream, as the tomatoes add flavour and moisture. Grill 2 streaky bacon rashers until crisp. Cut into small pieces. Hard boil 2 eggs and mash lightly in a bowl. Finely chop 2 ripe tomatoes and add to the egg with the bacon. Mix together and then spoon onto your chosen bread.

egg with red pepper & cucumber

Hard boil an egg and lightly mash it in a bowl. Add ¼ red pepper (finely chopped) to the bowl and a little finely chopped cucumber. Mix well, then spoon onto your chosen bread. You can thinly slice the pepper and cucumber if preferred.

how to hard boil an egg

Three-quarters fill a saucepan with water and bring to the boil. Carefully add an egg. Set the timer for 7 minutes (large eggs will need 8 minutes). Lift the egg out of the saucepan with a slotted spoon. Run cold water over the egg to stop it from cooking and to help cool it down. Peel away the shell.

Most children like to eat hard-boiled eggs plain and often like to peel away the shell themselves. They make a great little lunchbox filler. If your child likes to eat his/her egg with some dressing, include a little blob of salad cream or mayonnaise in a tub. Most brands of mayonnaise are made with pasteurized egg yolk, but always check the label. Add some bread and vegetable sticks to eat alongside the egg, and your child's packed lunch is ready.

nutrition tip Poor diet has been linked to problems such as learning difficulties, hyperactivity, attention deficit hyperactive disorder (ADHD), depression, stress and anxiety. It is therefore important that you offer your child a varied and healthy diet.

fish sandwiches

Fish is something that children love or hate, but it's a good idea to make sure they have some in their diet. Tuna is the easiest option, but some children also love sardines and salmon, both of which are good cupboard standbys.

note: Drain all tinned products before using.

tuna with mayonnaise & sweetcorn

This classic combination is liked by most children, and is very easy to make. Add a little mayonnaise to some tinned tuna with a handful of tinned or cooked sweetcorn, and mix everything together. Spread onto your chosen bread.

tuna with spring onion & tomato

Mix together half a tin of tuna with ¼ finely chopped spring onion and 1 finely chopped ripe tomato. Spread onto your chosen bread.

tuna with cream cheese & lettuce

Spread your chosen bread with cream cheese, top with a little tinned tuna and some shredded lettuce.

tuna with cucumber

Mash some tinned tuna, spread onto your chosen bread and top with thinly sliced cucumber. Alternatively, mix the tuna with a little finely chopped cucumber. Tinned salmon works well too.

salmon with tomato ketchup & cress

Mash some boned tinned red salmon with a little tomato ketchup. Spread onto wholemeal or granary bread and sprinkle with lots of mustard and cress (see page 13 on how to grow your own cress).

sardines, lemon & lettuce

Mash 2 tinned sardines with a little lemon juice and spread onto your chosen bread. Top with a handful of shredded lettuce.

prawns with mayonnaise & watercress

Prawns are a good occasional treat. If you are using frozen ones, leave to thaw first. Take a handful of cold cooked prawns and mix them with a little mayonnaise and natural yoghurt. Spread onto your chosen bread and top with watercress. This mixture is an acquired taste, but makes a great little sandwich filler.

creamy smoked mackerel

Skin and flake smoked mackerel fillets, then mix with a little mayonnaise and Greek yoghurt. Spread onto thick wholemeal bread and top with crisp lettuce leaves.

easy sandwiches

If you're in a hurry, these quick sandwiches are ideal for occasional treats. They are firm favourites with children, although Marmite is a spread they will either love or hate.

peanut butter & banana

Spread some peanut butter onto your chosen bread and top with a thinly sliced banana.

peanut butter with cucumber

Spread some peanut butter onto your chosen bread and top with thinly sliced cucumber.

peanut butter with grated carrot & raisins

Thinly spread some peanut butter onto your chosen bread and top with grated carrot and a handful of raisins.

jam & sliced banana

Spread some jam onto your chosen bread and top with sliced banana.

mashed banana & honey

Mash a banana with a little lemon juice to stop the banana from going brown, add a little honey and spread onto your chosen bread. Alternatively, spread a little honey in a roll and add the mashed banana.

Marmite & cheese

Lightly butter your chosen bread and thinly spread with Marmite. Sprinkle with a handful of grated Cheddar.

Marmite, cheese & cucumber

Spread some Marmite onto a small crusty baguette and top with grated cheese and thinly sliced cucumber.

one-pot salads

Try to vary between salads and sandwiches, so your child doesn't get bored with his/her lunch. You can add so many different things to couscous. It is a bit like pasta and changes flavour depending on the ingredients that you add to it. Don't forget to pop a spoon into the lunchbox with these salads.

couscous

couscous with feta

serves 2

100 g couscous

100 ml boiling stock or water

a handful of dried apricots (about 4–5), finely chopped

a handful of almonds, finely chopped

a small chunk of feta cheese (about 50 g), crumbled

a small handful of fresh mint, finely chopped, or 1 teaspoon mint sauce

couscous with tuna

serves 2

100 g couscous

100 ml boiling stock or water

½ tin tuna in sunflower oil, drained

a handful of black olives, finely chopped

4 cherry tomatoes, finely chopped

couscous with cucumber

serves 2

100 g couscous

100 ml boiling stock or water

¼ cucumber, finely diced

a handful of fresh mint, finely chopped

2 ripe tomatoes, finely chopped

dressing (for all 3 recipes):

freshly squeezed juice of ½ lemon

3 tablespoons olive oil

1 teaspoon honey

Put the couscous into a bowl, pour over the boiling stock, cover and leave for 10 minutes.

Once the grains of couscous have absorbed all the liquid, fluff them up with a fork. Add all the other ingredients (choose a recipe from the 3 provided) and mix together. Mix together the dressing ingredients and stir into the couscous. Keep chilled until ready to serve.

I always make these recipes for the whole family, hence why they both serve 4, but you can always cook half the amount or store half in the fridge for later. The Creamy Potato Salad is also good made with white cannellini beans instead of potatoes.

potato salads

creamy potato salad

serves 4

450 g new potatoes, halved

2 tablespoons mayonnaise

1 tablespoon natural yoghurt

a small handful of fresh mint or parsley, chopped

1–2 spring onions, finely chopped

2 handfuls of cubed cheese, chopped ham or bacon (for protein)

freshly ground black pepper

Bring a small pan of water to the boil, add the potatoes and boil for 10–12 minutes until just cooked. Drain.

Mix together the mayonnaise, yoghurt and herbs in a bowl. Season with a little black pepper. Add the potatoes, spring onions and cheese. Mix everything together, leave to cool and store in the fridge until needed.

potato, pesto & tuna salad

serves 4

450 g new potatoes, halved

2 large handfuls of green beans (about 150–175 g)

2 tablespoons green pesto

1 tablespoon olive oil

175 g tinned tuna in sunflower oil, drained

a handful of cherry tomatoes, halved

Bring a small pan of water to the boil, add the potatoes and boil for 10–12 minutes until just cooked. Trim the beans, cut in half and add to the potatoes 2 minutes before the end of cooking time. Drain.

Mix together the pesto and olive oil in a large bowl, add the potatoes and beans, tuna and tomatoes. Mix everything together, leave to cool and store in the fridge until needed.

My niece Clare often makes Red Pasta Salad for her lunch. It is a great recipe for using up leftover sausages. If you need to cook some sausages, try the sesame and honey recipe on page 73. Vary the type of pasta you use – little changes help to keep things more interesting for your child. Use brown pasta as often as possible, because it provides slow-release energy and fibre. I have used chipolata sausages, simply because they are thin and slice into good, bite-sized pieces. I have suggested that this recipe serves 2, so you can have some for your lunch too.

Jasmin, my middle daughter, thinks Tuna & Sweetcorn Pasta is the best packed lunch recipe ever! As with so many of the lunch ideas in this book, you can use this recipe as a guide and mix and match the ingredients.

> **great variation** Salmon and Pea Pasta is a tasty alternative to the Tuna and Sweetcorn Pasta. Make the recipe as per the Tuna and Sweetcorn Pasta, but use tinned salmon instead of tuna and cook some frozen or fresh peas instead of the sweetcorn.

pasta salads

red pasta salad

serves 2

100 g amori pasta shapes (or any of your choice)

3–4 teaspoons red pesto

4 teaspoons crème fraîche

2 chipolata sausages, cooked according to packet instructions and cooled

½ red pepper, deseeded and diced

6 cherry tomatoes, finely chopped

Bring a pan of water to the boil, add the pasta and cook according to the instructions on the packet. Drain and return to the pan.

In a small bowl, mix together the red pesto and crème fraîche.

Thinly slice the cooled sausages diagonally. Add the pepper, tomatoes and sausages to the pasta and tip in the pesto mixture. Mix everything together, leave to cool and store in the fridge until needed.

tuna & sweetcorn pasta

serves 2

100 g pasta spirals or penne (or any of your choice)

1 x 185-g tin tuna in sunflower oil, drained

1 x 200-g tin sweetcorn, drained and rinsed (or cook 200 g frozen or fresh sweetcorn)

1 tablespoon mayonnaise

1 tablespoon natural yoghurt

freshly ground black pepper

Bring a large pan of water to the boil, add the pasta and cook according to the instructions on the packet. Drain, put into a bowl and leave to cool.

Add the tuna and sweetcorn.

Mix together the mayonnaise and yoghurt with a little black pepper. Add the mayonnaise mixture to the pasta and mix together. Store in the fridge, ready to serve.

pick 'n' mix salad

Although this seems like a very simple recipe, it is important to encourage children to enjoy eating fresh vegetables, like cucumber, celery and carrots, which is why I have included this idea in my book. Given half the chance, my eldest daughter would choose to have Pick 'n' Mix Salad most days. Let your child help you decide what you put into the pick 'n' mix pot.

Put all the vegetables into a pot, and add the grapes, cheese and raisins. Store in the fridge ready to serve. This is best eaten with fingers. Pack a soft roll, some plain crackers or rice cakes with this salad to make a quick and easy lunch.

serves 2

¼ cucumber, cut into bite-sized chunks

2 sticks celery, cut into bite-sized chunks

2 carrots, peeled and cut into sticks

a handful of red grapes

a small piece of Cheddar (approximately 50 g), cut into bite-sized chunks

a handful of raisins

2 soft rolls, to serve

One small cabbage will make enough for about 4 portions of coleslaw. You may need to keep trying this recipe if your child turns his/her nose up the first time you give it to them.

You can be as creative with this recipe as you like – try adding grated apple (doused in lemon juice to stop it from going brown), beetroot, celery or red cabbage. Serve the vegetables thinly sliced so it's easier for children to eat and more appealing.

coleslaw

Cut the cabbage into quarters, cut out the hard core and then thinly slice the cabbage and put it into a bowl.

Add the carrots and pepper to the cabbage, along with the raisins. Add peanuts if you like.

In a small bowl, mix together the mayonnaise yoghurt and honey and season with a little black pepper. Add to the coleslaw and mix well. Store in the fridge, ready to serve.

nutrition tip If your child does not like eating cooked cabbage, making coleslaw is a good way of sneaking it into his/her diet.

serves 4

1 small head or ½ large white or green cabbage

2 carrots, peeled and grated

1 red pepper, deseeded and thinly sliced

a large handful of raisins

a large handful of peanuts (optional)

2 tablespoons mayonnaise or salad cream

1 tablespoon natural yoghurt

1 tablespoon runny honey

freshly ground black pepper

Many parents tell me that they just can't persuade their children to eat salad. One of the first pieces of advice I give them is to let their child make a dressing. Once children begin to mix and blend oils with vinegar or lemon juice and honey or garlic, they become quite excited about drizzling this over their greens.

You shouldn't think of green salads as boring – children can actually find the different textures and flavours quite interesting. From experience, the key to success is to make sure that the salad is interesting to look at and easy to eat (everything should be cut into small pieces).

green salad

serves 2

2 handfuls of crunchy lettuce leaves, washed and cut into small pieces

2 handfuls of baby spinach leaves or watercress, washed

optional extras

a small chunk of cucumber, thinly sliced

a large handful of green beans, trimmed and blanched

2 radishes (some children like the spiciness of these)

beetroot, sliced

carrot, peeled and grated

a large handful of seeds and nuts

dressing

3 tablespoons extra virgin olive oil

½–1 tablespoon lemon juice, white or red wine vinegar, or balsamic vinegar

with any of these:

1 tablespoon runny honey

½ small garlic clove, crushed

½ teaspoon mustard

Put the lettuce and baby spinach into a pot with a selection of the optional extras and mix together.

Make the dressing by mixing together the olive oil and lemon juice, and add more flavour with honey, garlic or mustard, if liked.

Pack the dressing separately in a small jar or pot, so your child can drizzle this onto the salad before eating. This will prevent the leaves from wilting.

You can make this recipe for an evening meal and then keep enough for a packed lunch the next day. Make sure you heat it through before you put it into the flask. Feel free to vary this recipe according to what you have in your store cupboard.

chicken & red pepper stew

2 tablespoons olive oil

8 boneless chicken thighs

2 onions, finely chopped

1 garlic clove, peeled and crushed

2 red peppers, deseeded and cut into bite-sized pieces

300 ml chicken or vegetable stock

1 x 400-g tin cannellini beans, drained and rinsed

freshly ground black pepper

a pinch of light soft brown sugar (optional)

serves 4

a heavy-based casserole dish

1. Preheat the oven to 180°C (350°F) gas 4. Heat half the oil in a heavy-based casserole dish, fry the chicken thighs until lightly browned all over and transfer to a plate.

2. Add the remaining oil to the casserole dish, then add the onions, garlic and red pepper and fry gently for 10–15 minutes until very soft, but not brown.

3. Add the stock to the mixture in the casserole dish and cook in the oven for 1 hour.

4. Spoon half of the sauce from the casserole dish into a jug and whiz with a hand-held blender until smooth. Put back into the pan.

5. Add the cannellini beans and chicken to the pan and cook for another 15 minutes until the chicken is cooked through. Cut the chicken into bite-sized pieces.

6. Season with black pepper and a pinch of light soft brown sugar, if you think it is needed. Serve for dinner and set some aside to cool for your child's lunch the next day. Wait until it has fully cooled, put in an airtight container and store in the fridge. Make sure you heat it through thoroughly before putting it in a flask.

This is my basic recipe for tomato soup. The key to success is first to choose ripe tomatoes, and secondly to leave them to stew for a while so that they reduce to a mush (this will help give the tomatoes an intense flavour). Most children love a creamy tomato soup, especially if you give them a fresh roll that they can dunk in it.

tomato soup

1 Heat the olive oil and butter in a saucepan, then fry the onion and garlic – this will take a good 10 minutes. You want them to soften, but not turn too brown. When the onion is soft, add the tomatoes and simmer gently, stirring occasionally until the tomatoes have turned to mush and most of the liquid has evaporated. This will take another 20 minutes.

2 Add the stock, bring to the boil, reduce the heat and simmer gently for 15 minutes.

3 Purée the soup with a hand-held blender or in a food processor. Return to the pan, warm through and add the sugar and black pepper.

4 If you want to make this soup really creamy, add a little cream or milk. Serve with a soft roll.

1 tablespoon olive oil

a knob of butter

1 onion, peeled and finely chopped

1 garlic clove, finely chopped

12 ripe tomatoes, halved

750 ml light chicken or vegetable stock

a pinch of light soft brown sugar

freshly ground black pepper

a little double cream (optional)

soft rolls, for dunking

serves 4

8 chipolata sausages

4 unsmoked (or lightly smoked) streaky bacon rashers

2 tablespoons olive oil

1 garlic clove, peeled and crushed

1 x 400-g tin chopped tomatoes

400 g tomato passata

450–550 ml chicken or vegetable stock (to achieve desired consistency)

2 x 400-g tins chickpeas, drained and rinsed

1 teaspoon light soft brown sugar (optional)

a handful of fresh thyme leaves, chopped

freshly ground black pepper

serves 4

If you are making this for a meal at home, you could also try adding some thinly sliced cabbage just before the end of cooking. It's best to avoid adding the cabbage if it is going to be taken to school in a flask, as it tends to go soggy with time.

If your child likes spicy food, try using chorizo sausage instead of chipolatas. Make sure that you keep all the pieces small, so that it is easy to eat.

sausage & bean casserole

1   Preheat the oven to 180°C (350°F) gas 4.

2   Roast the sausages for 25–30 minutes, turning occasionally until cooked through and golden. Slice diagonally into bite-sized pieces. Set to one side.

3   Snip the bacon into small pieces using a pair of scissors.

4   Heat the oil in a large heavy-based saucepan and fry the bacon until golden. Add the garlic and cook for 1 minute. Add the tomatoes, passata, stock, chickpeas, sausages, sugar, thyme and black pepper to taste, and simmer for another 20–25 minutes.

5   Serve for dinner and set some aside to cool for your child's lunch the next day. Wait until it has fully cooled, put in an airtight container and store in the fridge. Heat through thoroughly the next day before putting it in a flask.

The hint of sweetness in this butternut squash soup makes it appealing to children. To keep things as easy and quick as possible, roast the vegetables to bring out their sweetness and then purée them to make the soup. Add enough stock to suit your child's taste – some children find soup easier to eat if it is thicker in texture.

butternut squash soup

1 Preheat the oven to 190°C (375°F) gas 5.

2 Cut the butternut squash in half, scoop out the seeds and peel – you will need to use a sharp knife to cut the tough skin away. Cut the flesh into big pieces.

3 Put all the vegetables into a heavy-based roasting dish, add the garlic and drizzle over the oil – you may want to use your hands to mix everything together. Roast for 30–40 minutes.

4 Put the roasted vegetables into a food processor (squeeze the garlic out of the skins) with the stock – you may need to do this in two batches. Alternatively, blend with a hand-held blender. Purée until smooth.

5 Pour into a saucepan, season to taste with black pepper and a little honey. Heat gently.

For the Parmesan croutons: For the croutons, reduce the oven temperature to 180°C (350°F) gas 4. Put the diced bread into a roasting tray, drizzle with the oil and sprinkle with the Parmesan. Toss everything together. Put in the oven and roast for 5–10 minutes, turning occasionally, until light golden.

Put the croutons in a small airtight container or bag, so your child can add them to his/her soup at lunchtime. If you add them in the flask, they will dissolve into the soup.

1 butternut squash
(approximately 1.4 kg)

2 onions, cut into thin wedges

3 carrots, peeled and cut into thirds, widthways

2 sticks celery, cut in half

3 garlic cloves (unpeeled)

1 tablespoon olive oil

750 ml–1 litre boiling vegetable stock

freshly ground black pepper

a little honey

Parmesan croutons

3 thick slices of bread, diced

olive oil, for drizzling

Parmesan cheese, for sprinkling

serves 4

a heavy-based roasting dish

a food processor or hand-held blender

These noodles can be reheated the morning after you've made them and put in a flask, so that they're nice and hot for your child at lunchtime. Alternatively, you can serve them cold in an airtight container.

noodles

2 tablespoons red or white wine vinegar

4 tablespoons tomato purée

2 tablespoons light soft brown sugar

½ teaspoon mustard powder

1 teaspoon reduced salt soy sauce

4 bundles Chinese-style dried egg noodles or straight-to-wok noodles

2 teaspoons sunflower oil

2 teaspoons sesame oil

2 spring onions, thinly sliced

1 small garlic clove, peeled and crushed

2 handfuls each of sugar snap peas, baby corn, sliced green peppers

1 x 432-g tin pineapple pieces in juice

serves 4

1 In a bowl, mix together the vinegar, tomato purée, sugar, mustard powder and soy sauce. Set aside.

2 Bring a large pan of water to the boil and cook the noodles according to the packet instructions. Drain and set aside.

3 Heat the oils in a frying pan, add the spring onions, garlic and vegetables and stir-fry for a few minutes – you want them to be cooked, but still crisp.

4 Add the vinegar mixture and cook for a few minutes. Add the pineapple pieces and juice and continue to cook for a few more minutes until the liquid has reduced. Add the noodles and toss everything together.

5 Set the noodles aside to cool and store in the fridge, ready to serve.

cheese straws

This simple cheese pastry recipe is not only quick, but tasty. I tend to cut the straws into small lengths so that they don't break in the lunchbox. Depending on what you have available in your fridge, you can make the pastry with most cheeses – Red Leicester, Cheshire, Parmesan. Get your children to make these – they will love rubbing the butter into the flour and rolling out the pastry.

80 g plain flour, plus extra for dusting

40 g butter, chilled and cut into small pieces, plus extra for greasing

40 g strong Cheddar, grated

1 small egg, beaten

makes approximately 12

a baking tray, greased

(1) Preheat the oven to 180°C (350°F) gas 4. Sift the flour into a large bowl. Rub the butter into the flour using your fingertips until the mixture looks like fine breadcrumbs. Add the grated cheese and mix together.

(2) Add the beaten egg and stir into the flour until the mixture starts to come together. Then use your hands to work it into a ball.

(3) Sprinkle some flour onto the work surface and a rolling pin and roll out half the dough into a rectangle about ¼ cm thick. Cut widthways into straws. Carefully lift them onto the baking tray, leaving a little space between each one. Bake for 10 minutes, until golden.

(4) Leave the straws to cool for a couple of minutes on the tray and then carefully transfer them to a wire rack. Eat warm or leave to cool completely and store in an airtight container.

pesto cheese twists

This is a quick alternative to the Cheese Straws recipe. You can try these with Marmite or grainy mustard instead of the pesto if your child fancies something a little different. They are also suitable for freezing, so ideal for popping in your child's lunchbox as a quick fuss-free snack.

a little butter, for greasing

a little flour, for dusting

375 g ready-rolled puff pastry

about 80 g cheese, grated, e.g. Cheddar, Parmesan

2–3 tablespoons pesto or Marmite

makes 30

2 baking trays, greased

(1) Preheat the oven to 200°C (400°F) gas 6. Sprinkle the work surface with a little flour and spread out the pastry.

(2) Sprinkle the cheese evenly over half the pastry, then fold it in half. Using a rolling pin, roll the pastry out to its original size.

(3) Using a palette knife, spread the pesto over half of the pastry and fold in half. Roll out to its original size. Cut into long thin straws.

(4) Hold the end of a straw in one hand. Use your other hand to twist the other end of the straw to create a twisted shape. Lay it on a baking tray. Repeat with the other straws, leaving a little space between each one on the baking trays.

(5) Bake for 8–10 minutes.

(6) Remove from the oven, carefully lift the straws off the baking tray and put them onto a wire rack. Eat them warm or leave to cool completely and store in an airtight container.

Red peppers contain fantastic vitamins, like beta-carotene and vitamin C – both essential for helping boost immature immune systems. Try as often as possible to add vegetables to your child's favourite foods.

sausage & red pepper rolls

1 Preheat oven to 200°C (400°F) gas 6.

2 Dust your work surface with a little flour and roll out the pastry until it is approximately 30 cm x 28 cm and then cut in half lengthways.

3 Heat the oil in a frying pan, add the onion and pepper and sauté for 5 minutes or until soft. Add the chopped apple and cook for 1 minute. Leave to cool slightly.

4 Put the sausagemeat into a bowl, add the onion mixture and parsley (if using) and season with a little freshly ground black pepper and mix together.

5 Divide the sausagemeat mixture into two equal halves and shape each into a long sausage shape. Place each sausage shape along the long edge of each piece of pastry. Brush the opposite edge of the pastry with beaten egg and roll up from the sausagemeat edge. Seal the pastry edges and turn the rolls over so that the seam is underneath.

6 Cut each roll into 2.5-cm lengths. Cut a small slit in the top of each roll, brush with beaten egg and pop onto the baking sheets. Bake for 20–25 minutes. Remove from the oven, transfer to a wire rack and leave to cool.

plain flour, for dusting

375 g ready-rolled puff pastry

1 tablespoon olive oil

1 onion, finely chopped

1 red pepper, deseeded and finely chopped

1 apple, cored and finely chopped

450 g good-quality pork sausagemeat

1 handful fresh parsley, chopped (optional)

freshly ground black pepper

1 egg, beaten

makes 18–20

alternative filling

450 g chicken mince, 1 tablespoon honey and 2 teaspoons wholegrain mustard

2 large baking trays, greased

If your child likes cold pizza, why not make one to pop into his/her lunchbox? You can make these pizzas with rolls, muffins or French bread. Prepare these pizzas the night before – cook one for the lunchbox and keep the other in the fridge until you need it for your own lunch.

easy pizzas

2 English muffins or 1 thin part-baked French baguette

1 garlic clove

2–3 tablespoons tomato purée

toppings

salami, ham (shredded), tinned tuna in sunflower oil (drained), sweetcorn (drained), thinly sliced red pepper (deseeded), green or black olives (pitted and cut in half)

2 handfuls of grated Cheddar

6 slices mozzarella (optional)

serves 2

1 Preheat the oven to 190°C (375°F) gas 5.

2 Cut the muffin in half lengthways and lightly toast each half. Rub the cut side of each half with the garlic.

3 Spread the tomato purée over the muffin. Top with your child's favourite toppings, sprinkle with the Cheddar and lay the mozzarella on top, if using.

4 Cook in the oven for 5–8 minutes until golden and bubbling. Leave to cool.

This is a quick recipe idea for sausages –
great for lunchboxes, but also a big hit at
children's parties. You'll find that adults
love these just as much as children do.

sesame sausages

1 Preheat the oven to 200°C (400°F) gas 6. Twist
the sausages in the middle and then cut in half.

2 Scatter the sausages over a heavy-based
roasting dish and cook for 15–20 minutes,
turning once. Drain off any fat. Add the
honey and cook for another 15 minutes,
turning a couple of times until the sausages
are sticky and golden all over.

3 Sprinkle the sesame seeds over the sausages
and cook for a further 5 minutes.

12 good-quality chipolatas

2 tablespoons runny honey

2 tablespoons sesame seeds

a heavy-based roasting dish

serves 4

nutrition tip Most children need
small snacks in between meals
to help prevent blood sugar and
energy lows. Fresh fruits or
vegetables are ideal snacks, but
for those times when your child's
craving something a little bit more
filling, a small sesame sausage
can fill the gap.

Make these in the evening or at the weekend, when things are not quite so manic. Ask the children to help you to make the pastry – they love to rub the butter into the flour and roll and cut out the dough. Alternatively, buy some puff pastry and use this instead. Vary the fillings – try tuna and sweetcorn, chopped bacon (cooked) and cheese, and broccoli and salmon. Equally, if you don't have any double cream in your fridge, use another egg and a little more milk.

mini quiches

for the pastry:

225 g plain flour, plus extra for dusting

115 g butter, chilled and cut into small pieces

1 egg yolk

for the filling: 1 small onion, finely chopped (or 3 spring onions, finely chopped)

1 small garlic clove, crushed (optional)

1 tablespoon olive oil

1 egg, beaten

5 tablespoons double cream

5 tablespoons milk

2 skinless salmon fillets, cut into small cubes

a couple of handfuls finely grated Parmesan

makes 18

an 18-holed muffin tin, greased

1 Preheat the oven to 200°C (400°F) gas 6.

2 Sift the flour into a large mixing bowl, add the butter and egg and rub it in using your fingertips until the mixture looks like fine breadcrumbs.

3 Add 1–2 tablespoons water, a little at a time, stirring until the mixture comes together as a ball. Cover and chill for 30 minutes.

4 Sprinkle the work surface and your rolling pin with a little flour and roll the pastry out to about ¼ cm thick. Cut out circles to fit your muffin tin. Lay them in the muffin tin holes and prick the base of each tart once with a fork.

5 Bake for 5 minutes until the pastry is a very pale golden colour.

6 Gently fry the onion and garlic in the oil until soft.

7 In a jug, mix together the egg, cream and milk. Divide the onion mixture and salmon between the pastry cases. Drizzle over the egg mixture, sprinkle with the Parmesan and bake for 5–6 minutes until risen, slightly golden and set.

8 Remove from the oven and leave to cool for a few minutes before taking them out of the tin.

Cook these for supper and keep a couple in the fridge overnight ready for your child's lunchbox in the morning. Most children will enjoy nibbling the chicken off the bone, but if your child eats slowly, you might like to cut the chicken off the bone and pack it in a pot with a fork.

chicken drumsticks

1 Preheat the oven to 200°C (400°F) gas 6.

2 Score each piece of chicken about 2 or 3 times.

3 Put the onion into a large bowl, add all the other ingredients and mix well.

4 Add the chicken and stir really well until covered – you may prefer to use your hands to really work the marinade into the chicken. Cover and chill for 15–30 minutes.

5 Put the chicken into a heavy-based ovenproof dish and roast for 40–45 minutes. You may need to turn the chicken occasionally.

6 Leave to cool and keep in the fridge overnight, ready to pack in your child's lunchbox the next day.

8 chicken pieces (e.g. thighs, legs), skin removed

1 onion, peeled and finely chopped

8 tablespoons tomato ketchup

2 tablespoons soft dark brown sugar

1 tablespoon wholegrain mustard

1 tablespoon Worcestershire sauce

1 garlic clove, crushed

makes 4 (2 chicken pieces per serving)

a heavy-based ovenproof dish

My middle daughter has never really enjoyed eating sandwiches, unless they are cut very small and are easy to eat. She much prefers these puff pastry pinwheels. I have experimented with a whole variety of fillings, but this combination has been incredibly popular with children. If you don't have pesto in your cupboard, you can try them without.

puff pinwheels

4 unsmoked bacon rashers

1 tablespoon olive oil

2 spring onions, finely chopped

375 g ready-rolled puff pastry

2–3 tablespoons red pesto

100 g Cheddar, grated

makes 20

a baking tray

1 Preheat the oven to 190°C (375°F) gas 5. Cut the bacon into small pieces. Heat the oil in a frying pan and cook the bacon for 5–10 minutes, until cooked. Add the spring onions and cook gently until they are soft. Leave to cool slightly.

2 Unroll the pastry sheet, spread with the red pesto and scatter over the bacon and spring onions. Top with the grated Cheddar. Carefully roll the pastry, starting with a long side so that you end up with a long, thin sausage shape.

3 Cut the sausage shape into 20 circles and put onto a baking tray. Bake for 10–12 minutes until golden and risen. Remove from the oven and leave to cool on a wire rack.

great variation Another quick idea using puff pastry is to make Tuna and Sweetcorn mini pasties. Mix together a 185-g tin tuna, 2 handfuls cooked sweetcorn, and a little mayonnaise. Cut out approximately 20 circles from a sheet of 375 g ready-rolled puff pastry. Fill half the circle with the tuna mix. Fold the remaining half over the mixture and pinch the edges together to form a parcel. Put on a baking tray and bake in the oven (190°C (375°F) gas 5) until golden and cooked.

Leafy green vegetables, like spinach, contain omega-3, an important fatty acid that's known to help concentration. Spinach is also a good source of potassium, calcium and iron. Chop it up and add to omelettes, pasta sauces or fish pies – an effective way of getting your child to eat greens.

spinach & onion tortilla

1 Preheat the grill to high.

2 Break the eggs into a large bowl, season and beat briefly with a fork.

3 Heat the oil in a large frying pan with a heatproof handle and fry the onion until soft and pale golden. Add the spinach and sauté for a couple of minutes to wilt the leaves.

4 Pour the egg mixture into the pan, turn the heat down to its lowest setting and cook the tortilla, uncovered, for approximately 8 minutes, until there is only a little runny egg left on the top.

5 Sprinkle the grated cheese over the top and brown under the preheated grill for 1–2 minutes, until the top is golden and bubbling.

6 Use a palette knife to slide the tortilla out onto a plate. Cut into wedges. Leave to cool and store in the fridge, ready to serve.

5 eggs, beaten

sea salt and freshly ground black pepper

2 tablespoons olive oil

1 large Spanish onion, halved and thinly sliced

175 g fresh spinach leaves, washed and chopped

40 g Cheddar, grated

serves 4

Mackerel has the highest omega-3 content of all oily fish. Children need omega-3 for healthy brain function. Oily fish, like other fish, also contains essential minerals and protein and is a good source of vitamin D. You can serve this as a lunchbox snack in a couple of different ways. It can be used as a dip and eaten with vegetable sticks or fingers of toast, used to fill pita breads or rolls or spread onto tortilla wraps.

3 smoked mackerel fillets

125 ml (about 4 heaped tablespoons) natural yoghurt

1 garlic clove, peeled and roughly chopped

1 tablespoon wholegrain mustard or 1–2 tablespoons horseradish (optional)

freshly squeezed juice of ½ lemon

freshly ground black pepper

fingers of toast or vegetable sticks, to serve

makes 4 small tubs

a food processor or hand-held blender

> **nutrition tip** Mackerel is a great source of omega-3 essential fatty acids, which are associated with good brain development and mental health.

smoked mackerel pâté

1. Remove the skin from the mackerel fillets and flake the fish into a food processor (or into a bowl if using a hand-held blender).

2. Add the yoghurt, garlic, mustard and lemon juice and purée until smooth. Season with a little freshly ground black pepper, if liked.

3. Put the dip into small airtight tubs and store in the fridge, ready to serve. Cut up the desired number of vegetables or fingers to serve as an accompaniment. Store in the fridge and keep covered. It will keep for 2–3 days.

These scones are a great alternative to sandwiches – add some carrot or cucumber sticks and away you go! Make a batch and keep them in the freezer – put a frozen scone in your child's lunchbox in the morning and it will have thawed by lunchtime.

pick 'n' mix scones

1 Preheat the oven to 200°C (400°F) gas 6.

2 Sift the flour and baking powder into a large bowl. Add the butter and rub in until the mixture starts to look like fine breadcrumbs.

3 Add a handful each of 2 fillings of your choice. Use a knife to mix in the milk, a little at a time (you may not need to add all of it), until the mixture starts to come together.

4 Sprinkle a little flour onto your work surface, then tip the dough out of the bowl. Put a little flour on your hands and very lightly knead the mixture for ½ minute until it is smooth.

5 Form the mixture into a ball, and use your hands to lightly pat it out to about 3 cm thick. Dip a round cutter into a little flour and cut out scones from the dough. Put the scones onto the baking tray, spaced a little apart. Brush the tops of the scones with a little milk.

6 Bake for 8–10 minutes until risen and golden. Remove from the oven and leave the scones to cool on a wire rack. These freeze really well, so if you want to save some for later in the week, pop a few into some freezer bags.

225 g self-raising flour, plus extra for kneading

1 teaspoon baking powder

40 g butter, chilled and cut into small pieces

a handful each of 2 of the following: grated cheese, fresh herbs (finely chopped), sun-dried tomatoes (chopped), olives (pitted and cut in half), ham or bacon (chopped)

140–150 ml milk, plus a little extra for brushing

makes 8 large or 12 small scones

a round cutter

a baking tray, greased

snacks

pack a snack

which snacks to pack

Most young children need small snacks in between meals to help keep their energy levels up. Regular meals with snacks in between can help prevent blood sugar or energy lows. Schools encourage you to provide a snack for your child for the middle of the morning, and many schools have banned crisps and chocolate.

Fruits and vegetables are best, but sometimes children need something slightly more substantial, especially if they are playing a lot of sport or staying after school for a club.

If you are looking in the shops for snacks, be aware that many snacks marketed at children are often heavily refined and high in fat and sugar. These snacks not only lack a variety of important nutrients, but they are also likely to make children feel full, which can put them off eating their next meal.

keeping it fresh

Children 5 years and over need to be eating 5 servings of fresh fruit and vegetables per day to get plenty of vitamins, minerals, fibre and phytochemicals (plant nutrients) – all of which are essential for a healthy immune system, gut and heart.

good fruit

Each fruit contains different nutrients, so work hard to introduce new fruit into your child's diet. Bananas, apples, pears, oranges, plums, grapes, raspberries, strawberries, peaches and kiwi are all popular fruits for lunchboxes.

Encourage your child to try new fruits by doing the following:
- Cut kiwis in half and pack a spoon, so they can be eaten like a boiled egg!
- Cut oranges into quarters, so your child can suck the juice out – boys are often impressed to hear this is a popular snack at half-time among footballers!

good vegetables

Good vegetables for snacks include strips of raw peppers, cherry tomatoes, and carrot, celery or cucumber sticks.

snack ideas

rainbow pot

To help encourage your child to eat a variety of fruits and vegetables, fill an airtight pot with a colourful mix of his/her favourites. Use any fruits and vegetables (preferably seasonal) that you have to hand, and divide the pot up into quarters, putting red grapes, sticks of cucumber, slices of mango and slices of red pepper in each corner.

dried fruits

Be creative with your packaging and put raisins, apricots and mango into small bags and pots decorated with stickers. Let your child help – if he/she is excited about food, he/she will be more open to trying new things.

medley of mixed dried fruits

There are many dried fruits available, but the combination popular in our house is the medley of dried tropical fruits. Mix together some dried mango, pineapple and pawpaw in a small airtight pot. For a special treat, ask your child to help you half-dip some dried fruit in melted chocolate. Leave to dry and give them as a treat.

nuts & seeds

These contain beneficial monounsaturated fats and useful fibre, and are a great healthy snack option. Mix together a handful of dried fruits with some nuts and seeds and pop them in a small pot.

breadsticks, rice cakes or cheese biscuits

These are all great, especially with a chunk of cheese and a piece of fresh fruit, and are a good source of carbohydrate.

garlic pita crisps (see left)

A really simple recipe, children will love biting into these crispy little toasts.

serves 2

2 pita breads

olive oil

garlic clove, crushed

Cut the pita in half lengthways, cut each half widthways and then cut each quarter in half diagonally to make 8 triangles. Put the triangles on a baking tray, drizzle with a little oil and scatter over the garlic. Bake for 5–6 minutes until crisp and golden around the edges.

pieces of cheese

Babybel are often popular with children, partly, I am sure, because of the red waxy coating. Cheese is an excellent source of protein and calcium.

natural yoghurts with toppings

A small pot of yoghurt can fill a hungry hole and help keep your child happy until the next meal. If you are buying fruit yoghurts, check the label first. I have seen some yoghurts for children that contain 10 g of sugar in one pot (see page 10 for sugar intake information). For some great topping ideas, see page 102.

cereal bars

Look at the labels of so-called healthy cereal bars marketed at children – they often contain totally unacceptable levels of fat, salt and sugar (see pages 10–11 for information on sugar and salt intake). If you can set some time aside, it is much better to make your own cereal bars – see page 120.

nutrition tip Garlic is antiviral, antifungal and antibacterial. Children often love the taste of garlic and these crisps are quicker to eat than garlic bread.

Dips do not have to be complicated, and most children will be happy with a small pot of cream cheese and a handful of breadsticks for dipping. You will need to invest in a little pot, so your child can take the dips to school.

easy dips

cream cheese dip

Take 3 heaped tablespoons thick live natural yoghurt and mix with 2 tablespoons soft herb and garlic cream cheese (e.g. Boursin). Serve with pita crisps or vegetable sticks.

chickpea dip

There is very little point making a small portion of houmous, it is much better to make enough for a few people and keep it in the fridge until needed. You may enjoy eating this for your lunch too. It is easy to forget about eating good food yourself when you are busy looking after children.

serves 4

2 tablespoons sesame seeds

1 teaspoon ground cumin

400-g tin chickpeas, drained (approximately 240 g drained weight) and rinsed

1 garlic clove, finely chopped

freshly squeezed juice of 1 lemon

3 tablespoons olive oil

a handful of fresh coriander, chopped

freshly ground black pepper

to serve – a few sticks of vegetables (e.g. carrots, cucumber and celery)

Heat the sesame seeds and ground cumin in a dry frying pan for a minute to release their flavour, then put into a jug (or food processor). Add the chickpeas, garlic, lemon juice and oil and whiz to a purée.

Add the coriander and freshly ground black pepper and whiz again. If necessary, add a little more olive oil or water to make it your desired consistency.

Serve a small bowl of houmous with some vegetable sticks for dipping.

Bought popcorn can contain very high amounts of sugar. It is cheaper and healthier to make your own. Children are fascinated by the change in size and shape of corn kernels before and after they have popped – make sure you show them. Let them listen to the sound of the popping corn in the saucepan.

sweet popcorn

1. Put the oil into a large saucepan and heat until it is hot.

2. Tip the corn into the pan, and shake the pan gently so that the corn covers the entire saucepan base.

3. Cook the corn until it starts to pop, then put the lid on straight away. If you have a pan with a glass lid, it's fun for the kids to watch it pop.

4. Cook the corn for 2–3 more minutes. Hold the lid on tightly and shake it often. Keep cooking until the sound of popping corn stops.

5. Remove from the heat, take off the lid and pour over the sugar. Stir gently with a wooden spoon and tip into a serving bowl.

Other good things to add to popcorn: Vanilla sugar instead of ordinary sugar, or soft light brown sugar for a more toffee-like flavour, 1 tablespoon of golden syrup or maple syrup, or mix a pinch of cinnamon into your sugar. For savoury popcorn, try adding 50 g finely grated Cheddar or Parmesan.

2 tablespoons sunflower oil

65 g popping corn

1 dessertspoon golden caster sugar (optional)

serves 2

nutrition tip This is an ideal snack food as long as you **don't** add lots of sugar! Popcorn contains fibre and is low in fat, and is a much healthier snack alternative to crisps.

100 g Cheddar, grated

100 g butter, softened

125 g plain flour

1 teaspoon baking powder

1 tablespoon sunflower seeds

25 g puffed rice (breakfast cereal)

2 baking trays

makes approximately 20

> **nutrition tip** Cheese provides calcium, which is needed for building healthy bones. It is a good snack and the ideal alternative to pudding.

You can either give these as an alternative to sandwiches with some crunchy vegetable sticks, as a snack or serve with a piece of cheese and some fruit.

cheese & seed biscuits

1 Preheat the oven to 180°C (350°F) gas 4.

2 Line the baking trays with baking paper.

3 Put the cheese and butter in a mixing bowl. Add the flour, baking powder and seeds.

4 Put the puffed rice (breakfast cereal) into a plastic bag and use a rolling pin to bash the bag and break up the rice. Add to the bowl and mix everything together. This will take some time and you will need to use your hands.

5 Squeeze the mixture into small balls, about the size of cherry tomatoes. Put onto the baking trays and flatten slightly with a fork.

6 Bake for 10–15 minutes, until light golden. Carefully transfer them to a wire rack to cool.

7 Leave to cool completely, then store in an airtight container or freeze.

smoothie trio

I make these smoothies most mornings – they only take a couple of minutes. Just chop up any fruit that you have to hand, add some juice and blend. Use old fruit juice bottles and pack with a colourful straw. Use these basic recipes to start.

tropical mix

Pour 2 big glasses of orange or pineapple juice into a jug or food processor. Cut a mango either side of the stone, peel and roughly cut the flesh and add to the juice. Add a few pieces of tinned or fresh pineapple or 1 passion fruit and blend until smooth, either using a hand-held blender or in a food processor.

pink milk

This will need to be kept cold – invest in a good flask.

Pour 2 big glasses of milk into a jug. Add 1 ripe banana, 2 big handfuls of raspberries or strawberries and a little honey, then blend until smooth.

green juice

Pour 2 big glasses of apple juice into a jug or food processor, peel a ripe kiwi and cut the flesh into pieces, add to the juice with 1 peeled and roughly chopped banana. Blend until smooth using a hand-held blender or food processor. Chill all smoothies before serving.

nutrition tip Smoothies are easier to make than you might think and are a great way of encouraging your children to eat fruit, and even vegetables, as well as increase their fluid intake. They contain a large amount of natural sugar, so are great served alongside cereal or toast.

something sweet

yoghurt pots

You may, like me, be fed up with the high amount of sugar, additives and preservatives that can be found in so many of the yoghurts marketed at children.

I believe the best answer is to invest in some little plastic pots with tight-fitting lids and create your own yoghurts. It takes no time at all to spoon some natural yoghurt and a spoonful of jam or honey into a pot. Just don't forget to pack a spoon too. Adding your own flavourings to natural yoghurt can also work out to be much less expensive.

Natural bio yoghurt or probiotic yoghurt is best, because it contains friendly bacteria that are good for your child's gut. It is believed that the friendly bacteria can help to prevent constipation and diarrhoea as well as food poisoning.

It is also a good idea to pick full-fat yoghurt. Children do need some fat in their diet, and whole-milk natural yoghurt actually only contains 3 g fat per 100 g.

The following pages contain some ideas to get you started. Three-quarters fill your small pot with natural bio live yoghurt and top with one of the ideas listed to the right. When you add a topping to your natural yoghurt, try not to add too much or you could end up going over your child's daily sugar allowance (see page 11). Children don't need sugar, and should get used to the natural sweetness of dried fruit.

apricots & honey

Finely chop 3 dried apricots, and add to the yoghurt with 1 teaspoon runny honey.

jam with fresh fruit

Add 1 teaspoon fresh fruit jam to the yoghurt with a handful of fresh or frozen raspberries or other berries.

apple & raisins

Core and peel an eating apple, then grate it and mix with a tiny bit of lemon juice to stop it from going brown. Add to yoghurt with a handful of raisins or dried cranberries.

banana

Mash or finely chop 1 very ripe banana. You might like to mix it with a tiny bit of lemon juice to stop it from going brown. Add it to the yoghurt. If your child likes dates, add a few of these, chopped.

apple purée

Core and peel 4 dessert apples, cut into small pieces and put into a saucepan, add a tiny dribble of water and then cook gently until the apples are soft. Taste, and if they are really tart add a little light soft brown sugar. Add to the yoghurt. This will make enough for 3 or 4 portions.

muesli with honey

Sprinkle a handful of muesli on top of the yoghurt and drizzle with a little honey.

If you are going to make a cake, you may as well make a big one. At least that way it will last for a few packed lunches. People always comment on how moist this cake is. My secret is to add orange juice to the sultanas to make them plump and juicy.

sultana tray bake

1. Preheat the oven to 160°C (325°F) gas 3.

2. Put the sultanas in a saucepan and cover with orange juice. Bring to the boil, reduce the heat slightly and cook for 15 minutes or until all the juice has been absorbed by the sultanas.

3. Add the butter to the sultanas and stir gently over low heat until the butter has melted. Remove from the heat.

4. Mix the eggs, sugar and vanilla extract in a large mixing bowl.

5. Add the sultanas, flour and baking powder to the egg mixture and mix thoroughly. Pour into the roasting tin.

6. Bake for about 1 hour. You will need to check the cake after 40–45 minutes, when you may like to cover the top with baking parchment to stop it from going too brown.

7. Leave the cake in the tin for 5 minutes and then cut into about 24 squares. Dust with icing sugar.

450 g sultanas

260 ml (approximately) orange juice

250 g butter

3 eggs

350 g light soft brown sugar

2 teaspoons vanilla extract

350 g self-raising flour

1 teaspoon baking powder

golden icing sugar, to dust (optional)

makes about 24 squares

a 30 x 20-cm roasting tin, greased and base-lined

A finger of home-made shortbread with some fresh berries is an ideal pudding for a summer lunchbox. If your children are keen on lemon, then add the zest of 2 lemons instead of just the 1, for a real zing. Or if they prefer orange, try adding the zest from 1 orange instead.

lemon shortbread with berries

1 Preheat the oven to 190°C (375°F) gas 5.

2 Beat the butter and sugar together until soft, pale and fluffy.

3 Add the lemon zest, plain flour and cornflour and mix again until it comes together.

4 Cover the bowl and chill the mixture for 10 minutes, if you have the time. If not, you can cook it straight away – it will not make a big difference either way.

5 Press the dough into the prepared tin and bake for 15 minutes.

6 Remove from the oven and dust with sugar, if liked. Score the dough into about 12 fingers (score in half and then score each half into about 6 fingers) and leave to cool completely in the tin.

7 Once cool, cut into fingers and remove from the tin. Store in an airtight container.

175 g butter, softened

75 g golden caster sugar, plus extra to dust

zest of 1 unwaxed lemon

200 g plain flour

50 g cornflour

fresh seasonal fruit, to serve

makes 10–12 fingers

a 20-cm square tin, greased and base-lined

nutrition tip Whenever you give your child something sweet, like biscuits, cakes or shortbread, try to always offer some fresh fruit alongside to help boost their vitamin and mineral intake.

cranberry biscuits

You can make your own variations of these by adding other chopped dried fruits or chocolate. They will stay fresh in an airtight container for a week and also freeze really well. Biscuits should be crisp and firm, not gooey. Cookies, on the other hand, should be soft or chewy in the middle.

100 g butter, softened

100 g golden caster sugar

1 egg, beaten

½ teaspoon vanilla extract

280 g plain flour

50 g dried cranberries, raisins, chopped apricots or finely chopped milk chocolate

makes 30–32

a large baking tray, greased and base-lined

1. Preheat the oven to 180˚C (350˚F) gas 4.

2. Beat together the butter and sugar until pale and fluffy. Beat in the egg, then add the vanilla extract.

3. Add the flour and cranberries and mix together.

4. Use your hands to mould the mixture into a big ball.

5. Break the dough into three equal balls and roll each one into a log, about 10 cm in diameter. Slice each log into about 10 cookies. Put onto the baking tray and bake for 9–11 minutes or until just golden around the edges.

chocolate chip cookies

Get your children involved with this recipe – they will love mixing everything together and then spooning the mixture onto trays. These are a great alternative to a bar of chocolate.

75 g butter, softened

75 g light soft brown sugar

a few drops of vanilla extract

1 egg

2 tablespoons golden syrup

150 g self-raising flour

75 g chocolate, cut into small pieces or 75 g chocolate chips

makes 20

a large baking tray, greased and base-lined

1. Preheat the oven to 180˚C (350˚F) gas 4.

2. Cream the butter and sugar together until really soft. Add the vanilla extract and egg and beat again. Add the syrup and mix together.

3. Add the flour and mix together, then add the chocolate chunks and mix well.

4. Take small spoonfuls of the mixture and mould into balls about the size of walnuts.

5. Put on the baking tray, flatten their tops slightly with a knife or fork, and bake for 6 minutes. Remove from the oven and leave to cool. The cookies will continue to set as they cool.

muffins

I developed this recipe to make a tray of 12 muffins, so if you only need 6 you can freeze the other half for another week. It's nice to send your child to school with home-made bakes, especially if it's a recipe that's been in the family for generations, like this one. Experiment with different fruit; a little puréed pear or apple or mashed banana can be just as delicious as a handful of berries.

50 g butter (or sunflower oil)

300 g self-raising flour

2 teaspoons baking powder

80 g golden caster sugar

2 eggs

110 ml natural yoghurt (if you don't have yoghurt, you could use milk)

110 ml milk

a few drops of vanilla extract

2 big handfuls of berries (e.g. blueberries or raspberries)

makes 12

a 12-holed muffin tin

12 paper muffin cases

william's mini tarts

The classic sweet pastry I use in this recipe is light, crisp and easy to make. I use it for most of my sweet-based tarts and pies. My daughter's friend William came up with the idea of adding thinly sliced apple and golden syrup to the tart cases when he was making jam tarts one day. They really are delicious.

for the pastry:

225 g plain flour, plus extra for dusting

115 g butter, chilled and cut into small pieces

1 teaspoon golden caster sugar

1 egg yolk

1–2 tablespoons cold water

a biscuit cutter

an 18-holed tart tin, greased

makes 18

for the fillings:

for each mini apple tart:

a few slices of dessert apple

1–2 teaspoons golden syrup

for each mini lemon tart:

1–2 teaspoons lemon curd

for each mini jam tart:

1–2 teaspoons jam of your choice

for each mini sticky coconut tart:

1–2 teaspoons golden syrup

2 teaspoons shredded or desiccated coconut

1 Preheat the oven 200°C (400°F) gas 6. Line the 12 muffin holes with paper cases – if you don't have any, just grease the muffin holes really well with butter.

2 Melt the butter in the microwave or in a small pan. Leave to cool slightly. Sift the flour and baking powder in a large bowl. Add the sugar to the flour.

3 In a small bowl, whisk the eggs with a fork, add the yoghurt, milk, vanilla extract and melted butter.

4 Quickly and gently mix everything together in the large bowl. Don't over-mix or your muffins will not be light. Quickly fold in the fruit, and then spoon the mixture into the cases.

5 Bake for 25–30 minutes or until well risen and golden brown. Take the muffins out of the tin and leave to cool on a wire rack. When they have completely cooled, place in an airtight container, or you could bag, label, and freeze half for another time.

1 Sift the flour into a large mixing bowl, add the butter and rub it in using your fingertips until the mixture looks like fine breadcrumbs. Stir in the sugar. Use the knife to mix in the egg yolk, then add the water, a little at a time, stirring with the knife until the mixture comes together and you can form a ball with your hands.

2 Wrap the pastry in a piece of clingfilm and put it in the fridge for 30 minutes – this will make it easier to roll out.

3 Preheat the oven to 200°C (400°F) gas 6. Sprinkle the work surface and your rolling pin with a little flour and roll the pastry out to about ¼ cm thick. Dip the cutter in flour, then cut out as many circles as you can – you may need to gather up the bits of pastry and roll them out again to make 18 circles. Lay the rounds of pastry in the tart tin and press them gently into place. Prick the base of each tart once with a fork.

4 Put the tart tin into the oven. Bake for 6 minutes until the pastry is very pale golden. Remove from the oven. For the apple tarts, carefully put a few slices of dessert apple into each pastry case and drizzle with the syrup. Alternatively, add the filling of your choice and put the tin back into the oven for 6 minutes.

5 Remove from the oven. Leave the tarts to cool for a few minutes, then use a palette knife to gently lift them out of the tin. Leave to cool completely on a wire rack.

Jelly is something all children enjoy, so why not put some in their lunchbox as a tangy treat? Add some seasonal fresh fruits or tinned fruits into the pots before you pour over the jelly. You can also make the jelly with a combination of fruit juice and water.

fresh fruit jellies

orange jelly:

1 packet orange jelly

1 tin mandarins or fresh satsumas

raspberry jelly:

1 packet raspberry jelly

1 tin raspberries or fresh or frozen raspberries

lemon jelly:

1 packet lemon jelly

1 tin citrus fruits or fresh orange, peach or apricots

strawberry jelly:

1 packet strawberry jelly

fresh or frozen strawberries or raspberries

5–6 jelly moulds

makes each packet of jelly will make 5–6 small jellies

1 If you are using tinned fruits, melt the jelly with the recommended amount of water (usually 100 ml). Then add the juice from the tin of fruit and enough water to make it up to the right volume according to the packet instructions. If using fresh fruit, follow the packet instructions for the jelly.

2 Mash half the tinned or fresh fruit to a pulp and add to the jelly. Divide the remaining fruits between the jelly moulds. Pour the fruity jelly mixture over the fruit in each mould and leave to set overnight.

Sometimes all you need to do is change the packaging of food to entice children to start eating it. Some children find a variety of fresh fruit chopped and mixed together in a pot more appealing than eating whole individual fruits. Mixing familiar fruit with something new can be a great way to introduce different fruit to your child's diet.

little pots of fresh fruits

 ### kiwi & satsuma

Peel the skin off a kiwi using a sharp knife and cut the flesh into bite-sized chunks. Peel a satsuma and mix the segments with the kiwi chunks in an airtight container.

pineapple & mango

Tropical fruits are often popular with children. Cut them into big pieces that they can hold or small pieces that they can eat with a fork. Peel and cut a pineapple into bite-sized chunks. Put a handful in an airtight container and store the rest in the fridge for later. Peel and cut half a mango into bite-sized chunks. Put a handful into the airtight container of pineapple and mix together. Store the other half in the fridge for later.

grapes & pear

Core a pear and cut into bite-sized chunks, then sprinkle with a little freshly squeezed lemon juice to prevent it from turning brown. Put the pears into a pot and add a handful of grapes.

nutrition tip Sometimes it is easier to eat fruit that is chopped up and ready to eat, but try to vary this with whole fruit so that children become used to eating fruit straight from the tree. Children should be eating 5 a day!

As a busy mum, I often bake 2 cakes at the same time and pop one in the freezer to eat a week later. It takes exactly the same amount of time to make 2 of these gingerbread cakes as it does 1. Alternatively, this cake mix can be baked in one 25-cm-round cake tin, but it will need to cook for 1½ hours.

225 g butter

225 g dark muscovado sugar

225 g black treacle

2 eggs, beaten

340 g plain flour

2 teaspoons ground cinnamon

1 tablespoon ground ginger

1 teaspoon bicarbonate of soda

285 ml warm milk

makes 2 x 2 lb loaf loaves

2 x 2-lb loaf tins, greased and base-lined

sticky gingerbread

1. Preheat the oven to 140°C (275°F) gas 1.

2. Line the 2 loaf tins with a paper loaf tin liner.

3. Put the butter, sugar and treacle into a large saucepan and heat gently, stirring constantly until melted.

4. Remove from the heat, leave to cool slightly and then stir in the beaten eggs.

5. Sift the flour, cinnamon and ginger into the melted mixture.

6. Mix together the bicarbonate of soda and warm milk. Add to the ginger mixture, mix well and pour equal amounts of the mixture into each tin.

7. Bake for just under 1 hour. The top of the cake will be slightly golden with a lovely crust and a skewer should come out clean.

chocolate cupcakes

These are ideal for a Friday treat. There are many ways to decorate mini cupcakes – let your children decide how.

175 g unsalted butter, softened

175 g golden caster sugar

3 large eggs, beaten

175 g self-raising flour (minus 2 tablespoons)

2 tablespoons cocoa powder

2 tablespoons milk

200 g icing sugar

pink food colouring

chocolate buttons, to decorate

2 x small 12-holed muffin tins

24 paper cases

makes 24 mini cakes

1. Preheat the oven to 180°C (350°F) gas 4.

2. Put the paper cases into the holes of the mini muffin trays. Cream together the butter and sugar until pale and fluffy. Gradually add the eggs, one at a time, beating well after each addition.

3. Fold the flour and cocoa powder into the mixture. Then mix in the milk, so that the mixture drops easily from the spoon. Fill the paper cases with spoonfuls of the mixture. Bake for 10 minutes. Remove from the oven and leave to cool on a wire rack.

4. Sift the icing sugar into a bowl and mix with a little hot water until it creates a thick pouring consistency. Add the pink food colouring and mix.

5. Spread a little icing over the cakes and decorate with chocolate buttons. Leave to set. Store in an airtight container.

mini pear cakes

These cakes are very quick to make and freeze brilliantly. Make sure the pears are nice and ripe before making this recipe.

1 ripe pear or 1 eating apple

125 ml vegetable oil

1 egg

75 g golden caster sugar, plus extra for dusting

150 g self-raising flour (you can use all white or try half white and half wholemeal)

ground cinnamon, for dusting

2 x small 12-holed muffin tins, greased

makes 24 mini pear cakes

1. Peel the pear, halve, core and then cut into small pieces.

2. Put the oil, egg and sugar in a bowl and whisk them together.

3. Add the flour and the pear and quickly mix everything together.

4. Almost fill each muffin hole with the mixture and then bake for 12–15 minutes until risen and light golden.

5. Remove from the oven, take the pear cakes out of the tin, and dust with the cinnamon and leave to cool on a wire rack.

muesli cookies

Muesli is a good mix of carbohydrates (oats), protein (nuts) and vitamins (dried fruit), and tastes great in these sweet cookies.

175 g butter

3 tablespoons runny honey

225 g muesli

200 g self-raising flour

50 g light soft brown sugar

2 large baking trays, greased and base-lined

makes about 20

1. Preheat the oven to 180°C (350°F) gas 4.

2. Melt the butter and honey in a saucepan, then remove from the heat.

3. Put the muesli, flour and sugar into a large bowl and then add the butter mixture. Mix well.

4. Spoon spoonfuls of the mixture, spaced apart, onto the lined baking tray. Bake for 10–15 minutes or until golden.

5. Remove from the oven, lift them off the baking trays and leave to cool on a wire rack.

fruity flapjacks

I only ever make large batches of flapjacks because they are very popular in my family. If they don't all get grabbed up after baking, store half in the freezer for lunchbox snacks.

80 g light soft brown sugar

180 g butter

150 g golden syrup

300 g porridge oats

75 g dried apricots, finely chopped (try to buy unsulphured ones if you can)

a 30 x 20-cm roasting tin, greased and base-lined

makes 12

1. Preheat the oven to 180°C (350°F) gas 4.

2. Put the sugar, butter and golden syrup into a pan. Heat gently over low heat until the sugar has dissolved.

3. Take the pan off the heat and add the oats and apricots. Mix well.

4. Tip the mixture into the prepared tin and spread it out evenly right to the edges. Use the back of the spoon to smooth the top. Bake for 18–20 minutes, until golden and cooked.

5. Remove from the oven and leave the flapjacks to cool for 5 minutes.

6. While the flapjacks are still warm, use a knife to mark them into squares. Leave them to cool completely on a wire rack. Cut them into squares along the score marks and store them in an airtight container.

cereal bars

100 ml sunflower oil

30 g light soft brown sugar

150 ml golden syrup

250 g rolled oats

100 g mixture of seeds (e.g. sunflower seeds, pumpkin seeds)

60 g dried fruits (e.g. raisins, cranberries or chopped apricots)

makes 16

a 20-cm-square tin, greased

1) Preheat the oven to 180°C (350°F) gas 4.

2) Put the oil, sugar and syrup into a pan and heat very gently to dissolve the sugar.

3) Add the rest of the ingredients and mix well. Tip into the greased tin and bake for 15–18 minutes until set and golden.

4) Leave to cool for 10 minutes, and then score into 16 bars.

5) Leave to cool completely in the tin, turn out and cut along the marks into 16 bars.

6) Store in an airtight container.

nutrition tip Oats are a great source of fibre and long-lasting energy. The seeds are a fantastic source of protein and the dried fruit contains essential vitamins.

Dried fruit is a great source of fibre and I would strongly recommend having a stash in your storecupboard.

apricot slices

1 Preheat the oven to 180°C (350°F) gas 4.

2 Put the dried apricots and orange juice into a small saucepan. Simmer gently for about 15 minutes until all the juice has been absorbed by the apricots (they should be soft and sticky).

3 Put the oil and honey into another saucepan and heat gently until the honey dissolves into the oil. Add the oats and flour to the oil and mix.

4 Put half of the oat mix into the tin and press down. Cover with apricots – make sure that you cover the oats with the apricots. Spread the remaining oat mixture over the top of the apricots to cover.

5 Bake for 20–25 minutes until golden on the top. Remove from the oven and score into 16 slices while still warm. Once cooled, cut the bars along the score lines and store in an airtight container.

225 g dried apricots (try to buy unsulphured ones if you can), finely chopped

approximately 6 tablespoons orange juice – you may need to add a little more during cooking

175 ml sunflower oil

4 tablespoons runny honey

175 g oats

175 g plain flour (or a mixture of wholemeal and plain flour)

a 20-cm-square tin, greased and base-lined

makes 16

packaging

Keep it fresh

Some of the fresh food ideas in this book, like pâtés, cooked chicken and yoghurts, will need to be kept cool in the lunchbox. If you can, purchase an insulated lunchbox. Alternatively, add a small icepack to your child's lunchbox to help keep the contents fresh.

Similarly, any hot food will need to be kept hot, so it's good to invest in a good flask. The small fat ones are best for children, because they can eat straight from them without having to decant the food into a bowl.

Recycle

Once you start to make healthy lunchboxes for your child, you'll discover that you create less waste because you are no longer purchasing heavily packaged products.

When you make your child's packed lunch, try to keep the amount of packaging you use to a minimum and recycle anything left in the lunchbox. Involve your children by asking them to put their rubbish into the relevant bins, so that they get used to the idea of recycling. Remember rubbish in the bin means more rubbish in the landfill site, and this is what we must avoid.

Try to avoid using clingfilm, foil, plastic sandwich bags and mixed packaging (e.g. drink cartons). These materials are not suitable for recycling (with the occasional exception of foil) and even though the sandwich bags could be reused, they have a short lifetime and will end up in the bin sooner than a plastic tub.

What should I use to store food in a lunchbox?

You should try to reuse things that you already have in your kitchen. You could even use an old ice cream container as a lunchbox.

Small pots

Collect little airtight containers or pots that dips, pasta sauces or olives come in and keep them to store lunchbox snacks. You can also put yoghurt into small pots and wash them after using (just make sure the lid is airtight, so the yoghurt doesn't leak out). If you buy individual yoghurts, wash out the pots and keep them so your children can use them for craft projects.

Tin pots with plastic lids

Keep your eyes open for bargain containers, like metal ones with plastic lids that can be reused.

Paper bags and greaseproof paper

Buy big packets of things, like biscuits, rather than buying them individually wrapped. Similarly, avoid packaged cheese slices. Instead, wrap up food like biscuits and cheese in paper bags or greaseproof paper.

Ready-made packaging

Some food, especially items of fruit, like plums, apples, and oranges, come pre-packaged when they could easily be sold loose. Try to buy fruit from your local market to avoid this unecessary packaging. If you are going to chop fruit into bite-sized pieces, put them into small pots.

Bottles

When you buy juice or water in small bottles, keep them so you can use them to store water and home-made smoothies. Try to avoid buying drinks in cartons because these are made from at least 3 materials – card, foil and plastic – and cannot be recycled as the process is too expensive.

Where your food comes from

Make your children aware of food miles by showing them on an atlas where their food has travelled from. The country of origin will usually appear on the packaging. Who has the packed lunch with the most food miles? Is it necessary to buy New Zealand apples when farmers grow them locally? Get your child to think about how they could have an altogether 'greener' packed lunch?

Fair trade

Many people in other countries work hard to produce the food we eat, yet they rarely get paid enough to feed their families. Next time you're in a supermarket, have a look at fair trade products like fresh fruit, yoghurt, honey, sugar and jam and think about why we should try to buy these wherever possible.

menu planner

To help you on your way to producing healthy lunchboxes for your children, use this weekly menu planner as a starting point. As you prepare the lunches, think of how you can package them without creating excess waste.

monday

- turkey with cranberry sauce and lettuce wrap (see page 31)
- a handful of vegetable sticks
- a handful of dried fruits
- a piece of cheese and a cheese biscuit
- a drink of water

tuesday

- tuna and sweetcorn pasta (see page 44)
- fresh peach – cut into quarters
- a fruity flapjack (see page 118)
- a drink of milk

wednesday

- egg mayonnaise and watercress sandwich (see page 32)
- a banana
- natural yoghurt mixed with a little honey or fruit topping (see page 102)
- a drink of fruit juice

thursday

- a sardine, lemon and lettuce sandwich (see page 35)
- a handful of nuts and seeds
- a kiwi cut in half (with spoon for scooping out flesh)
- a smoothie (see page 99)

friday

- butternut squash soup with Parmesan croutons (see page 61)
- yoghurt with a little honey or fruit topping (see page 102)
- a satsuma
- 2 x muesli cookies (see page 118)
- a drink of water

index

acknowledgements

Thank you David for your love and trust, and to Ella, Lola and Finley, my three biggest pickles in the pickle jar. Thanks Pop and Liz for being there. Mavis, I treasure our chats about food, recipes and life. Thanks to Marcus and James for the fond memories and inspiration for the recipes.

Thanks to Vicki for helping create another exciting project, one that Lara and the Lara all-stars can enjoy.

Thanks to Alison, Iona and Catherine and everyone involved in this book from Ryland Peters and Small.

Tara, I wished we lived closer, thanks for heading out of London so many times and for all the beautiful photos. Thanks to Chloe for your advice about rabbits and Liz for all the lunchboxes!

Brenda, thanks for your enthusiasm, help and laughs, you look GOOD in a skirt and you are a great assistant!

Thanks to Annie from the Northmoor Trust, and the lovely Eka Morgan.

Well done to the models Ella, Lola & Finley; Sadie & Angus; Rory; Annabelle & Thomas; Violet; Ollie; Jemima; Liliana & Saskia; Biba; Erin; Hector; Matthew; Kitty; Ilaina & Huwaida. I hope you enjoy making and packing your own lunchboxes.

Amanda Grant